GLADYS AYLWARD

Missionary to China

Sam Wellman

BARBOUR
PUBLISHING, INC.
Uhrichsville, Ohio

Other books in the "Heroes of the Faith" series:

Brother Andrew
Corrie ten Boom
William and Catherine Booth
John Bunyan
William Carey
Amy Carmichael
George Washington Carver
Fanny Crosby
Frederick Douglass
Jonathan Edwards
Jim Elliot
Charles Finney
Billy Graham
C. S. Lewis
Eric Liddell

David Livingstone
Martin Luther
D. L. Moody
Samuel Morris
George Müller
Watchman Nee
John Newton
Florence Nightingale
Mary Slessor
Charles Spurgeon
Hudson Taylor
Mother Teresa
Sojourner Truth
John Wesley

©MCMXCVIII by Sam Wellman

ISBN 1-57748-222-0

Published by Barbour Publishing, Inc., P.O. Box 719, Uhrichsville, Ohio 44683 http://www.barbourbooks.com

Cover illustration © Dick Bobnick.

Member of the
Evangelical Christian
Publishers Association

Printed in the United States of America.

GLADYS AYLWARD

one

Gladys Aylward sat in a hard, high-backed chair across from a spare desk. The office was well lit but drafty, and the dark, wintry bleakness of London outside made the window reflect her face like a mirror. She trembled at her image. Such a pitiful little mouse. Yes, she certainly looked like a mouse with luminous dark eyes and a sharp, prominent nose. Did she hear the hardwood floors creaking outside the door?

"Forgive me, God," she mumbled under her breath.

Anxiety gnawed on her. Did it mean she didn't trust God? Surely God would forgive her. Who wouldn't be rattled after being summoned out of the middle of a theology class at the Women's Training Center of the China Inland Mission? Did she hear someone outside the room? Yes! The creaking of the hardwood hallway grew louder and louder. . . .

"Oh no. Please, God. . ."

The door opened. "Miss Gladys Aylward." The voice of the Center's principal sounded hollow.

Gladys gulped and nodded. Where was her courage? The tall man sat down behind the desk heavily. His face was stone. Its coldness sent chills to Gladys's heart. She saw now he held a folder. Surely it contained her records at the Center. He opened the folder. She thought she saw him take a deep breath.

"China became very receptive to missionaries in 1928 when Chiang Kai-shek became President. So, Miss Aylward, we've begun a great effort to increase our mission staffs there by twenty percent." He paused and blinked. The corners of his mouth seemed to curl down in self-reproach. Had he suddenly realized that his touting this great opportunity would make rejection even more bitter for Gladys? His next words were hammer blows, "It's about your record. . . ."

"It's been a good ten years since I attended Silver Street School in Edmonton, sir," she blurted, adding almost hysterically, "I don't remember ever passing a test there."

"You're too modest, Miss Aylward. We know your record there was satisfactory. Besides, this meeting is not about your record at Silver Street School. This is about your record here at the Center. After all, you've been with us now for three months. . ."

"Yes, sir, and it's been a dream come true."

He set his jaw. Her gratitude seemed to unnerve him. "It's not that you don't assimilate the material taught you. You do. It just seems that you're starting well behind the others. Very far behind, in fact. Your instructors tell me that no less than three years will be required for you to bring yourself up to the level of competence we demand of our

6

missionaries before we send them out."

"Then I'm willing to take those three years, sir."

He blinked. Had he wanted to roll his eyes? "I'm sure you are willing, Miss Aylward. It's just that by the time you reach the level of competence we desire for our missionaries you will be almost thirty years old." He rushed on to prevent her from another show of willingness. "Everyone here agrees it is nearly impossible to learn the Chinese language at that advanced age."

"But. . ." The sentence died in her throat. "Nothing, sir."

The famous missionary David Livingstone was twenty-eight when he mastered Bechuana in South Africa. Another famous missionary, Mary Slessor, was about the same age when she mastered the Efik language in Nigeria. Both these great missionaries learned very difficult tonal languages at nearly thirty years of age. Should Gladys protest by mentioning their stories?

No. If she had learned nothing else in all her years as a parlor maid it was when to speak to authority and when not to speak. Besides, this poor principal seemed to be skirting a larger objection to Gladys. He was sparing her feelings, she was sure. What was it about her? Her slowness at learning? Her apparent timidity? Her apparent softness? Whatever it was, they had lost confidence in her.

Was her great dream of becoming a missionary to China really over? Then why had she gone one night several years ago to a revival in a church, not particularly moved but curious enough to go back later to the church to seek advice? Why had the pastor not been there, yet his wife had counseled Gladys? Why, under the wife's sober instruction, had God been reborn in her? Why had the longing to go to China risen inside her like a calling? Why, God, delude a poor, simple, uneducated working girl? Why? Why? Why? Her great dream of becoming a missionary to China was over. That reality struck at her heart like an icy dagger.

"You have a wonderful work record, Miss Aylward," said the principal brightly.

"I won't go back into service, sir," she said obstinately.

But that vow was nothing but pure stubbornness. What choice did she have? She had to work. She couldn't just go home to Edmonton in north London to live with Dad and Mum. That just wasn't done. She couldn't even go home to live with them while she worked. In service one had to live in the manor night and day. Of course, she was still young enough to have prospects of marriage. So what if she hadn't yet met a man who was serious and devout? It wasn't as if such a man didn't exist. She was no prize herself but she was healthy and hard-working. But in the meantime she had to work. Oh, how she dreaded going back into service. It wasn't just the shame before her own people of having failed. It was the shame before God of serving a few rich people when she could have served so many of the needy.

"Perhaps you can help the mission cause yet," mulled the principal.

"Yes, I'll go to China as an assistant!" she quickly volunteered. "I'll do anything. I'll. . ."

"I meant you could help us here in Britain. We have a missionary couple returning from China to retire in Bristol. They are elderly. They will need assistance."

"Oh, I don't. . ." Gladys paused. No one who read the

Bible like she had did not know how complicated God's plan can be for even the righteous. Who could not marvel at the way Abraham was tested? Or Paul? All through the Holy Bible. And all though history after that. Did John Bunyan give up the gospel when threatened with endless days in prison? No, he endured an unheated cell in Bedford for twelve years. So why should Gladys consider serving two retired missionaries beyond her endurance?

"I will be glad to be of service, sir," she concluded. Fighting back tears, Gladys even managed a smile.

two

Gladys was shrouded in gloom as she packed her belongings at the Women's Training Home in Highbury. She had come there months ago from her parlor maid's job in central London, past the Marble Arch, past King's Cross, up Pentonville Road, past an old shopping square called the "Angel." Oh, how high her spirits had been then. As high, mind you, as they were low now as she headed to her parents' home in Edmonton.

"A failure," she muttered.

It was only her Mum's bubbly optimism that kept her afloat until she traveled to Bristol by train. Rolling west across the lovely green shires of southern England to Bristol should have been a wonderful adventure, but Gladys was gloomy. Then she remembered John Wesley had made the same trip over a hundred years before and he had been gloomy about his prospects too. But his meeting in Bristol with George Whitefield changed his life—and Britain's. From a refined, even dandified, Anglican Church pastor

Wesley became a preaching firebrand of the outdoors—and Britain was never the same again. But who was meek Gladys Aylward to compare herself with John Wesley?

"You must learn to trust God with all your heart and soul, Gladys," urged the male half of the retired missionary couple in Bristol after she arrived. "You came here to Bristol with doubt in your heart. Listen with your heart and mind and He will give you some sign."

"But how?"

"Read your Bible. Pray with fervor. Talk to people who serve Christ. Serve Christ yourself!"

Bristol was not joy or fulfillment for Gladys, but it was certainly enlightening. Under the elderly couple's sagacity she began to learn about the real China too—not the rosy images painted by the China Inland Mission to recruit missionaries, but the blackness of the real China: the throwing away of girl babies like trash, the binding of women's feet into crippled clubs, the sickening arrogance of men taking more than one wife. The plight of women in China was an abomination. And the condition of men was not much better. This old couple had seen it all and they didn't mind telling Gladys about it.

Did they do it to harm the missionary effort? Not at all. "Quite the opposite!" stormed the old missionaries.

Gladys knew exactly what they meant. The horrors of China demanded the love of Christ. And it was the wife who soon sized up Gladys and told her about herself. "You've too big a heart to waste on just two old fools who think they are righteous anyway. We're going to find you a spot where you can help the lost."

"Yes, we'll not slow this young warrior down," added

11

her husband. "She must move on!"

Whether it was the old man or the old woman or Gladys who arrived at the conclusion Christ would be better served by Gladys moving on into "Rescue" work was hard to say. Certainly Gladys herself, except for the privilege of hearing the missionary couple talk about China, thought she was wasted in Bristol. But all three were so immersed in local evangelism as well as correspondence everywhere—yes, Gladys too, because she read and wrote letters for them—that it was hard to know when or how or from whom the city of Swansea beckoned Gladys.

She had hardly got to know the great port city of Bristol. It swarmed with church history. Bristol's cathedral was nearly eight hundred years old. The bowling green at Pithay was where George Whitefield dragged reluctant John Wesley on April 1, 1739, to hear his first "field preaching." At a brickyard on Saint Phillip's Plain Wesley himself field-preached the next day. Near the Horse Fair Wesley built the first Methodist chapel. But Gladys was not a spectator.

"I must serve Christ myself," she told the old couple's approving faces as she left.

Swansea, a port city also, was fifty miles due west of Bristol. For a young lady from north London it was a bit like foreign mission work. For Swansea was in Wales with its musical but tongue-twisting Welsh language that, to Gladys anyway, seemed to be missing half the consonants found in the English language. Besides the Welsh-speaking villagers who came down from the coal-laden mountain valleys to the port, there were sailors from all over the globe. And Gladys began to discern phrases of Spanish, Portuguese, Greek, Russian, German, Dutch and French.

Her work was at the Sunshine Hostel. She was far too small to confront the burly sailors lurching drunkenly from the taverns infesting the docks. No, as assistant matron it was her mission to rescue the women who drank with the sailors. At first she keyed in on the youngest ones, many of whom had just come to Swansea. For them it was not too late. Gladys would shepherd them back to the mission hostel where they were sobered up and put to bed. If there was time they were regaled with sermons and hymns at the Snellings Gospel Mission. Next morning the young ladies were given fare to return home. Once in a while Gladys would challenge older women. Occasionally she could get one to go to the Snellings Gospel Mission with her, perhaps more out of fatigue than remorse. For these "fallen women" were nearly always back in the taverns the next evening.

"I enjoyed the hymns, honey," many would say in heavy-accented English, just one of many languages of commerce they had learned.

But the thought of China began to haunt Gladys. She saved not a penny in her work in Swansea. What little she had she routinely gave away to young ladies too penniless to get home without her help. This generosity nagged at Gladys, for she had begun to dream of getting to China on her own. The old couple had planted the seed. Women outlived men in China as well as everywhere else in the world. And China teemed with elderly women missionaries, so the old couple said. If only Gladys could get there, surely there would be an elderly woman missionary who would welcome her assistance.

"Then who knows what great things would follow?" she told herself hopefully.

Nevertheless, Gladys endured Swansea. She endured the depressing frequency of vomit on her uniform. She endured the difficulty of trying to penetrate drunken brains with righteousness. She endured seeing the old prostitutes go back to sin again and again, yet knowing she not only had to forgive them again and again but try to rescue them again and again. She endured the danger, even though Gladys discovered that trusting God made her fearless most of the time. She endured the drunken sailors who tried to paw her. She endured the pervading sin of the docks, because Gladys knew the Lord had gone straight to sinners Himself.

She also endured the weather with its sameness. Unlike London, the summer days were never sunny nor did they reach seventy-five degrees. And in winter, the days were never freezing cold, with hard flakes of snow blowing like leaves. No, in Swansea it rained two days out of three.

So what finally pushed Gladys beyond her endurance of Swansea? "China!" she blurted one day upon reading a letter from a former employer.

Gladys had put the word out among her friends in great manors and her friends doing churchwork: she was willing to go to China even as a nanny if necessary, or at last resort she would work in a good manor so she could save money to go to China on her own. So it was no surprise one of her many contacts had written her of an opening for a parlor maid. Gladys had a reputation in service. She always belittled herself as "not very smart but quick and willing," but the letter said the wife of Sir Francis Younghusband wanted someone dependable, someone who could really help the house-keeper, someone who could manage the under parlor maids.

14

The letter said Gladys fit those requirements perfectly. There was an underlying motive, Gladys was sure; probably her former employer wanted to ingratiate herself to the Younghusbands. And Gladys would never have been enticed with flattery anyway, whether she suspected it was true or not. No, the thing that grabbed her was the reputation of Sir Francis Younghusband. Unsaid in the letter was that years ago, Colonel Francis Younghusband had led British expeditions through the perilous Mustagh Pass and over old silk routes into Tibet and. . .

"China!" gasped Gladys. Her heart beat faster and faster as she speculated. A knighted gentleman like Sir Francis Younghusband would have quite a library on China. She was sure of that. If she quickly proved herself, milady would probably let her read his books. And the Younghusbands would pay a handsome salary too. Perhaps twenty pounds sterling a year. And if Gladys saved her salary, worked extra parties on her days off and such, maybe even sold her belongings too, why who knew how soon she could afford passage to China?

Her heart beat faster just thinking about it. Once in China she would offer her assistance to any one of a flock of aging missionaries. The rest would be pure joy in serving Christ. She went over it again and again in her mind. It all seemed quite plausible. And soon it was all settled in her mind.

"Nothing can keep me from leaving Swansea now," she told herself with determination.

Gladys had seen little of what was touted as scenic around Swansea. The fashionable resorts of Oystermouth and The Mumbles were pointed out to her in the distance.

15

Ancient Oystermouth castle she saw not at all. Even more remote was the scenic valley that ran up from Neath into the Brecon Beacons—even though she had worked for the Christian Association of Women and Girls in Neath for a short time. "Oh, the Neath Valley with its grand gorges and spewing waterfalls will snatch your breath away," everyone told her. But Gladys saw none of it. She would remember her short, dull work in Neath. She would certainly remember her hard work for the Sunshine Hostel in Swansea. She would remember Snellings Gospel Mission with its singing and comfort. She would remember the docks with their seedy night life. She would remember the smoke roiling up from the great steel mills to the southeast. She would remember the rain. But most of all, she would remember reading the letter from her former employer and the burst of joy at her remembrance of the site of one of Sir Francis Younghusband's adventures.

"China!"

three

"My goodness," muttered Gladys as she stopped to survey her new manor in London.

For years she had worked in service in London's West End. West Enders considered themselves the very heart and soul of London. A few would have haughtily added "and all of England," perhaps even added "and all of the British Empire!" Still, it was no wonder. The West End stretched from the Houses of Parliament on the Thames River all the way west beyond Kensington Palace and Notting Hill. Kensington, the Strand, Hyde Park, Buckingham Palace, Picadilly, the British Museum, Mayfair, the National Gallery, Westminster Abbey, Trafalgar Square—all were claimed by the West End. This had been Gladys's world for many years.

"But this," she marveled as she contemplated her new manor. "Am I ready for this?"

For her new manor was in Belgrave Square. The elegance

of the Belgrave Square area was rivaled in London only by the Mayfair area. Palatial three-story residences of yellow brick and white columns framed the square. Tasteful fences and gates of black wrought-iron separated the manors from the wide walkways. It was London at its most sumptuous, if one chose to regard Buckingham Palace—itself no more than a three-minute stroll away down Chapel Street—as not relevant to normal human beings.

Gladys could not believe her good fortune. "I've been secured as the new house parlor maid," she told the footman who answered the bell at the servant's entrance.

The footman was slightly taken aback. Gladys had assumed her very best Oxford accent. As a child she had dreamed night and day of being on the stage. In spite of her physical shortcomings—tiny stature and timid-looking face—she had been in school plays. She had become a splendid mimic. Years of service to her betters had trained her to speak pure "Oxonian" any time it was required. In service it helped. It was intimidating. The footman could not hide his puzzlement all the while he took Gladys to the butler. But by the time he found the butler his attitude had changed to resentment.

"Sir, 'er royal 'ighness 'ere is reportin' for 'er coronation," he seethed in his best cockney accent.

In the upstairs bedroom the butler assigned her, Gladys was struck by doubt. The smallness of the room seemed crushing. All the rigid rules of service came flooding over her. A servant must be seen as seldom as possible by her betters. A servant never speaks to a better unless she is spoken to first. Even the servants themselves had a hierarchy. Only senior servants like the butler or the housekeeper could speak before the vegetables were served at the servants' dinner in their own quarters. She sensed her loss of freedom.

Was she deluding herself about China? How could she ever save enough money? After twelve years as a domestic servant she had few possessions. At her parents' home in Edmonton was her "bottom drawer" or "hope chest," her accumulation of fine things for marriage like a silver service, embroidered linens, and a lace tablecloth. Here in Belgrave Square, praise God, she had at least her well-worn Bible—but little else. And how much money? She opened her purse over the bed. Copper coins plinked together on the spread.

"Two pennies and one half penny!" she groaned. And anguish cried from her, "Oh God, I possess almost nothing. But here's my Bible. Here's my money. And here's me! Use me, God!"

Moments later a maid—wide-eyed from overhearing Gladys—poked her head in the door to say that milady, the mistress of the household, wanted to see Gladys in the drawing room.

There Gladys met Lady Younghusband, a plump, dough-faced woman of about seventy.

"Please inform me, Miss Aylward, whose task it is to clean the mirrors in the drawing room."

"I believe it is the task of the footman, or perhaps, the second footman."

"Quite right. Although at my grandfather Hollingsworth Magniac's Chesterfield House it was the *fifth* footman," sniffed milady.

Lady Younghusband became more amiable as she

digested Gladys's refined accent. Milady's attitude was contemptible, but Gladys had served far worse. Milady even gave her three shillings to offset any expense getting to Belgrave Square.

On the way to see the housekeeper to have her duties explained to her, Gladys glanced into the library. Thousands of leather-bound volumes loomed there invitingly. With three shillings in her pocket and the prospect of harvesting information about China from the library, Gladys was glowing.

Surely God has already answered my cry: Use me!, she thought.

Gladys soon learned the Younghusbands were not the permanent residents. The manor belonged to one of milady's brothers. The Younghusbands, who had a manor in Westerham about thirty miles south of London, were simply enjoying the convenience of London for a while. Although the staff was an assembly of odd sorts, the manor on Belgrave Square ran like a well-oiled machine. The butler, the housekeeper and the cook were military in their demands. Each servant not only had to do their duties thoroughly, but precisely *when* required. Long before the betters arose, the servants scurried about stoking fireplaces and stoves, ironing the morning newspapers, then delivering morning trays of coffee to their betters' bedroom suites.

The staff's main charges were Sir Francis, milady and their daughter Eileen, who appeared to be about thirty years old. While the betters rose and dressed, with the help of their lady's maid or valet of course, the other servants busily laid out breakfast and did everything else necessary for the first meal. Then while the betters dined, served by the butler and the footman, the other servants rushed to the upper floors to make beds and clean the bedrooms and bathrooms.

Custom was so rigid, Gladys wore a dress of pale lilac in the morning, indicating she was a housemaid. In the afternoon she wore the black dress of a parlor maid. Also required were white apron and cap, black stockings, and boots. In spite of her refinement, a maid like Gladys was to be seen as seldom as possible by her betters. If she were never seen at all she was judged absolute perfection itself. A perfect maid could go unacknowledged by the master of the manor for years at a time. All day, except for those who directly attended their betters, the servants busied themselves—always one step ahead of the betters. The very demanding work didn't let up until after the final evening meal.

"Until tomorrow then," said the butler stuffily as he eyed his pocket watch.

There certainly weren't enough hours left in the day to do everything Gladys wanted to do. She very discretely borrowed Sir Francis Younghusband's books—the old gentleman seemed always in the library writing something— and read late into the night. It was rare when she didn't fall asleep with a book in her hands. He had brought from Westerham his fabulous collection of books on Asia. First, she read of Sir Francis's exploits, as often as not described in books written by himself. His travels through Manchuria, the Gobi desert, the Himalayan Mountains and the high plateaus called the Pamirs he detailed in *The Heart of a Continent* in 1896. In 1904 he entered the Forbidden City of Lhasa in Tibet. It was this mystical-sounding adventure that made his reputation.

"Famous throughout the British Empire," sniffed the housekeeper.

In 1910 Sir Francis described in *India and Tibet* his expedition that "conquered" the Forbidden City as well as the events leading up to his venture. His zeal for that part of the world seemed endless. He also wrote in 1917, *Kashmir,* in 1921 a book on the Sikhim Himalayas titled *The Heart of Nature,* and in 1926 *Epic of Mount Everest.* That was not enough for the man. He also wrote a novel *But In Our Lives,* which some of the servants gossiped about. Gladys had no interest in such a book. In view of his Asian adventures among contemplative monks it was no surprise to Gladys to learn he was also deeply involved in mysticism. Gladys would have loved to question Sir Francis about his way of meeting God.

"But I dare not bother such a busy gentleman to inquire just how he does it," she told herself.

In *The Heart of a Continent,* although she was disturbed by his assessment of the Chinese, Gladys was cheered to learn Sir Francis greatly admired the courage of missionaries in China. For he had written:

> *It must be a stern, true heart indeed which*
> *can stand the dreary years spent almost—*
> *sometimes quite—alone in a remote Chinese*
> *town, far away from all the glamour and catch-*
> *ing enthusiasm of a missionary meeting at*
> *home, and surrounded by cold-blooded, unemo-*
> *tional Chinamen who by instinct hate you. . . .*

Because he had such admiration for missionaries she was not surprised he possessed the final accounts of missionaries like *Hudson Taylor and the China Inland Mission,* Marshall Broomhall's *Jubilee Story of the China Inland Mission,* Richard Timothy's *Forty-five Years in China* and A. E. Moule's *Half a Century in China.* The earlier exploits of missionaries like *Fire and Sword in Shansi* he had in his collection too. Gladys also bolstered herself with books written by women missionaries: *The Story of the China Inland Mission* by Geraldine Guiness, *Among Hills and Valleys of Western China* by Hannah Davies, *The Yangtze Valley and Beyond* by Isabella Bird, and *Behind the Great Wall* by Irene Barnes. Never again would Gladys doubt that women played a key role in the missionary work in China.

"And so shall I," said a determined Gladys, quickly adding, "If God wills it for me."

She boned up on the recent history of China too. The Manchus had been overthrown in 1911. Since that time China had been in turmoil. The soul of the new China was born in the patriot Sun Yat-sen and his political party, the "Kuomintang," or "Nationalists." But Sun Yat-sen had not the soldiers to hold China. China was divided among several great warlords, who still held power. Since Sun Yat-sen's death his protégé, Chiang Kai-shek, had emerged to unite a fragile alliance of warlords into a national government. But China was not even remotely a republic. Under the great warlords were thousands of Mandarins, who held absolute authority over their small districts.

Gladys also studied her Bible. Hadn't the missionary couple in Bristol told her that was one way God would guide her? Certain passages struck her too. They seemed to speak directly to her. God's words in Genesis 12:1 resonated with her heart and soul:

> *Get thee out of thy country, and from thy kindred, and from thy father's house, unto a land that I will show thee. . . .*

Thus God spoke to Abraham, and Abraham obeyed. Faith. Trust. And Moses had the same faith. The patriarch could barely express himself to others, yet God chose him. And Moses kept the faith. To Gladys's surprise the book of Nehemiah struck a very strong chord with her. Nehemiah wanted to serve God, but instead, as a cupbearer, he served the king—just as Gladys wanted to serve God but instead, as a parlor maid, served her "betters." Nehemiah wanted to go to Jerusalem to help the exiles returning from Babylon rebuild the city. But first he had to be released from his duties to the king. He prayed for God's help, then succeeded. After that introduction, Gladys was always especially fond of the book of Nehemiah.

Never had God spoken to Gladys as He now seemed to from the Bible. So she studied her Bible as never before. Besides, she soon would be delivering the gospel to the heathen, wouldn't she?

As if she didn't have enough to do, she began "field-preaching." Not in Belgrave Square, of course. Her employers would have been mortified. But other places nearby—where the Younghusbands' great Rolls Royce automobile would not venture past—she would preach right on the sidewalk. She startled more than a few bowler-hatted men scurrying by her with umbrellas and newspapers. Hyde Park nearby was a favorite place for orators of every kind. There Gladys stood on the proverbial soapbox and told men and women in a more curious mood the good news of Jesus Christ. Hyde Park was also a favorite place for hecklers. It was a real test for her. In spite of her timid appearance Gladys became very effective on her feet. She learned to parry almost every thrust. Some days she seemed invincible. And at times she was too proud.

"But after all," she told herself, to avoid becoming conceited, "I have the ultimate truth on my side. I only have to learn how to deliver it."

Invariably she stopped in Hyde Park to preach on Fridays. That was the day she also rushed along Picadilly to the Haymarket where Mullers' Travel Agency was located. For there Gladys was making payments on her fare to China. They hadn't wanted to sell her a ticket at all.

"But you don't understand, Miss," the travel agent had groaned. "Train travel to China by the overland route through Russia is not possible right now." He became truly obstinate only after he decided the commonness of her clothing took precedent over her superior accent.

"But I can't afford seafare," she countered logically. "It's twice the cost of a rail ticket."

The travel agent patiently explained why she could not take the train from London to Hull, take a ship across the North Sea to the Hague in Holland, then take the train all the way across Russia, then continue on through Manchuria to the port of Dairen on the China Sea. There a steamer would take her to the Chinese port city of Tientsin, he said, if she made it to Dairen, which she could not. The

Chinese were fighting the Russians on the very border between Russia and Manchuria.

"I've heard of no such war," she objected.

"It is precisely over control of the eastern end of the railroad—the part that goes through Manchuria—that they are fighting," he emphasized. "Some Chinese warlord they call the 'Young Marshall.' "

"That would be Chang Hsueh-liang," she amplified.

"His name could be Chop Suey for all I care," he fumed. "The point is—there is fighting going on."

"I'm a woman," she told him logically. "They wouldn't hurt a woman."

"We do not want our customers—especially young women—to reach their destination dead!" he spouted.

"Please take this on account," purred Gladys, pushing some money toward him.

Gladys could tell the travel agent was biting his tongue. His face seemed about to explode. But suddenly his face softened. He had realized her down payment was a mere three pounds sterling. She would need fifteen times that amount to complete payment on a ticket. He studied her attire. She was obviously in service somewhere. Even senior servants earned not much more than about twenty pounds a year. This Miss Aylward, he must have been reasoning to himself, would never be able to completely pay for the fare.

Looking more chipper, he wrote on a pad. "Here's a receipt, Miss Aylward, for your magnanimous down payment," he said with a knowing look.

The travel agent was not Gladys's only skeptic. She did not live in a vacuum. There was a sizable staff serving the

Younghusbands. The butler was too clever by far to pass any judgment on Gladys. He had seen the way milady was impressed by Gladys. Nor did the housekeeper or the cook judge her. These were senior servants, old hands who knew the worm could turn.

Of course Lady Younghusband's personal maid was far too discrete to show her feelings. The scullery maids were too inferior to Gladys in the world of domestics to openly judge her. But the rest of the younger staff was not so prudent. The footman teased Gladys relentlessly. The chauffeur thought she was insane. And the under parlor maids, who had to answer to Gladys, nevertheless didn't bother to hide their feelings that Gladys was either a silly dreamer or deranged. In their inexperience they had assessed her as one who would never rise to the level of a senior servant.

" 'Ousekeeper?" said one too loudly. " 'Er? Never."

One peculiar thing about a manor was that the servants were too busy all day to socialize much among themselves, nor did they ever have the opportunity to socialize together outside the manor. The time off they were granted was never at the same time. So they socialized with friends from other manors, often in other districts of London. In fact Gladys knew many other parlor maids in London's West End. But even old friends from other manors who called her "Glad" were now no source of pleasure to Gladys. For in their friendship they inadvertently diverted her from her plan to go to China.

"They are 'trouping the color' for the king, Glad," enthused one of her friends. "Let's go watch for the princes. Perhaps we'll see Prince Edward."

"Some young gents offered to take us for a cruise on

the Serpentine in Hyde Park," said one maid. "Come with us, Glad."

"There's a new Alfred Hitchcock talkie called *Murder* at the moving pictures, Glad," offered another. "It's even better than *Blackmail,* his first talkie."

"Let's go shopping, Glad," tempted another one. "They're selling the new radio sets so cheap now. Think of the free concerts we can listen to."

"I've just borrowed the most wonderful new Agatha Christie mystery, Glad. Come, let's read it together."

"Glad, there's a Shakespeare Festival over at the. . ."

Plays, mystery books, talkies, radios, royalty. The truth was that London—the western world, in fact—never offered more distractions. Gladys was born the year the great Italian tenor Enrico Caruso made his first phonograph recording, and the amusements possible to those who had a little money had only increased every year. Her friends were only being human. But Gladys had no time for amusements. And she now tried outside of work to make all her human contacts in some way serve Christ. Her few chitchats were with workers in various church organizations. Some were acquaintances from the China Inland Mission Center. Some were acquaintances from other mission societies. One day in early 1930 was memorable.

"Poor old Jeannie Lawson, Glad," said a friend at a Methodist Church auxiliary. "She's seventy-three. The old missionary tried to retire here in England last year but it was too tame for her, I guess. The old dear felt compelled to return to China."

"How interesting."

Her friend grinned. "One of Jeannie's friends got a letter

recently. The old dear is afraid no one will carry on her work. Seems Jeannie is begging for an assistant."

"Then why doesn't the mission society send her one?" asked Gladys, her heart pounding.

"She's tried for years to get help. It seems the help must come not at all—or come unofficially. . ."

"That's me!" gasped Gladys.

"You might want her address then."

Gladys wrote Jeannie Lawson at once to offer her assistance. Then after much prayer she resolved to go ahead just as if Jeannie Lawson had already written back with her approval. This was surely God's plan for her, reasoned Gladys. And she must trust God. She applied for a passport. She changed her emphasis: There was no time to read about China now. No time to preach. Every free moment must be spent raising money. She was far short of the money needed for her rail ticket across Russia. She must put the word out that she was available for extra duty outside her manor.

It would surely help her cause to be employed in such a prestigious manor. Sir Francis hobnobbed with bluebloods like the Winston Churchills and Lord Kitchener. Sir Francis knew personally world figures as diverse as Cecil Rhodes, Mahatma Ghandi, and the poet Yeats. So it was not so hard to spread the word. If another manor needed someone to help with a party, Gladys was available. If it was an all-night party, so much the better. Upper crust revelers, glowing from a night of celebrating, paid best of all. If help was needed with a banquet, Gladys was available. House work, kitchen work, garden work. Gladys was available. She began selling all the nice things out of her hope

29

chest. She proceeded as if Jeannie Lawson would surely accept her offer of help. . .

"God willing," she admitted.

One day at the Younghusband manor on Belgrave Square the butler distributed the mail to the servants after their dinner. He paused and blinked at one wispy envelope festooned with bright hieroglyphic stamps. "What's this?" He frowned. "Japanese? Chinese? For Gladys?"

"China!" gasped one the other parlor maids.

"She probably ordered some blooming firecrackers," sneered the footman.

But he stared at Gladys expectantly. So did the butler, the cook, the housekeeper, the lady's maid, the valet, the chauffeur, the scullery maids, and the other parlor maids. Gladys scarcely had to read the return address to know the letter was from Jeannie Lawson. Who else would write her from China?

When she held the letter in her trembling fingers and saw it was indeed from Jeannie Lawson, she was not enraptured but seized with doubt. What if the letter contained Jeannie Lawson's polite refusal of her offer of assistance? How could she have been so presumptuous? One did not presume God would do this or do that. One could only hope to understand His will and follow it.

"Well, blimey, aren't you going to open the letter?" blurted the footman.

"What's the hurry?" answered Gladys breezily.

But she felt sick. She could not bring herself to open the letter in front of the others. All through the cleanup of their employers' dinner, she felt sick. Her life hung in the balance. Was her life going to be an adventure of joy or secure drudgery? She returned to her bedroom numb. Her hands felt like blocks of wood as she fumbled with the wispy letter.

She could barely steady the letter enough to read the words.

four

Gladys steadied her hands. She had to read her letter from Jeannie Lawson twice to make sure she read it correctly.

"Yes!" she finally gasped. "I must only reach Tientsin on the coast of China and Jeannie Lawson will send someone to guide me!"

The next months were a blur. Somehow, through the grace of God she was sure, Gladys raised enough money to pay for the ticket. On the day of her departure from the manor, the Younghusband staff reacted in amazement that she was actually leaving in a few days on the train for China. Even the footman had nothing more to say than a sober "I suppose it's good luck to you then." Milady was quizzical but imperious. The daughter Eileen looked worried. Gladys had learned Eileen was a bit of a rebel, savoring the company of radical friends from the London School of Economics, friends milady considered "low-life." What was Eileen thinking? Was she wondering if she had the courage to do what Gladys was doing?

"Or does she think me a fool?" Gladys wondered.

Once Gladys thought the steely blue eyes in the beetle-browed, walrus-mustached face of the aloof Sir Francis were studying her. After all, hadn't he written in *The Heart of a Continent* that "the hearts of all true Englishmen and all true Christian nations ought to go out to encouraging and helping those who have given up everything in this life to do good to others"? Yet his look of curiosity disappeared in a twinkling. Surely this encouragement and help did not extend to tiny unqualified parlor maids!

A few days later her parents and sister Violet were on the subway, accompanying her from Edmonton to the Liverpool Street Railway Station, north of the Tower of London. Her brother Lawrence could not get leave from the military to see her off.

"Seems odd you can take a train to China," mumbled Dad, who looked sick with worry.

"Three weeks and I'll bc thcrc, Dad!" gushed Gladys.

"Won't it be winter in Russia?" he fretted.

"I'll be on the train, Dad!"

Dad was so shaken he excused himself at the Bethnal Green Station. Couldn't get off work, he explained feebly. The other two Aylwards helped Gladys install herself in a third-class compartment on the train. Gladys had packed two suitcases. One contained her clothing. Her Mum donated a corset, not for wearing, but for stowing valuables. No decent person would investigate such intimate apparel, reasoned Mum. Hidden inside were Gladys's Bible, passport, various rail tickets, and two pounds sterling worth of travelers' checks. In addition to that money Gladys carried a few coppers. Mum also donated the kettle, one saucepan, and a tiny alcohol stove Gladys had tied to the suitcase full of food. For in the second suitcase Gladys had crammed cans of sardines, corned beef, and beans, as well as jars of bouillon cubes and powdered coffee. Very carefully, she had added hard-boiled eggs and packets of cookies and crackers.

"You won't starve," commented Violet, trying unsuccessfully to sound nonchalant.

"I'm ready for any kind of weather too," chirped Gladys as she tucked up around her neck a fur wrap her mother had tailored for her out of an old fur coat.

But the farewells made her heart ache. After the train had pulled out, she buried her face in the wrap and let the tears flow. Would she ever see her Mum and Dad again? Sister Violet? Brother Lawrence? England? She found her Bible. The Word of God soothed her pain. And prayer calmed her.

The train rolled straight north. It was October 18, 1930, and the countryside was blanketed by freshly-plowed, new-seeded fields. She crossed half of the east of England before she left the train at Hull to board a ship.

Away from the thicket of cranes and masts rising in the docks of Hull, the ship entered the swelling energy of the North Sea. Gladys fought seasickness all the way to the Hague in Holland.

After she disembarked, she was taken to the train station, where once again she was installed in a compartment in the choice window seat facing the engine. Her few coppers were gone but she began to relax. She would be in Russia, so the travel agency said, before she changed trains again. Russian trains ran on a narrower gauge track.

"Is Russia so different?" she wondered.

But first Gladys had to cross Germany, which she found different enough. Germany was peculiarly unfriendly. Officials entered her compartment on the train and asked impertinent questions. Was she actually born in England? Was she Jewish? Why was she going into Russia? Was she a Communist? They had the queer look about them Gladys had seen on servants who were trying to impress those beneath them by acting very superior.

But Germany was soon behind her, and she watched deep-pitched roofs of Polish farmhouses. Then came Russia and its narrow-gauged railroad tracks. Still, the change from one train to another in Russia was as simple as lugging her bags a few steps across a platform. But as the train moved on toward Moscow, Gladys saw how deceptive that simple change was.

"Russia is very different," she admitted to herself after a few days.

The Communist political system was not popular among Gladys or her church friends, but English intellectuals favored it. Here she saw its reality. The Russian people looked desperately poor. They were just as cheerless as the Germans but in contrast to the Germans' air of great expectations, the Russians exuded hopelessness. It was hard for Gladys to be objective, because the Russian men were crude beyond her experience. It wasn't just that they were unshaven and filthy. Nor was it because they smelled of many weeks of sweat. But they spat everywhere. They blew their noses with their fingers. They scratched themselves shamelessly. She was appalled and disgusted at their primitive behavior. It was frightening. It seemed beyond any crudity in the ancient world of the Bible. In fact, she reflected, she might be seeing the first fruits of a Godless society. Did these men have no notion at all as to how to behave?

"Or are these barbaric men left over from the czarist days?" she asked herself, trying to be objective.

But she knew she wanted no part of Russia. She was startled by the thought: *What if the Chinese are this barbaric?* What had she done?

Near Moscow was the heartbreaking sight of work gangs of small children. They were working along the railway track in freezing weather. The misery of Russia made Gladys brood. For the first time she felt homesick, not for Belgrave Square, but for her parents' home in Edmonton.

Their small red-brick and gray-stone house was at 67 Cheddington Road. It was so far north of London proper she could see open fields out their lace-curtained windows. Beyond their white-flowered privet hedge, horse-drawn carts clopped on the street of gray cobblestone, their drivers hawking milk, greens, bread, and a dozen other things. Rosalind, her mum, would bustle about the kitchen when she wasn't at the missions haranguing the evil of alcohol. Thomas, her dad, would clomp in at nightfall in his heavy boots and dark, red-piped postman's uniform.

At least that was the way home had been in her earliest years. It wasn't so serene when London—one of the most populated cities in the world—crowded in all around Cheddington Road and brought smoke-spewing automobiles and trucks.

"Still I've nothing but fond memories of Edmonton,"

she reminded herself.

Even the air raids of the Great War were pure gold to her now. The great German zeppelins—dirigibles, some blokes called them—would appear in the sky, floating in the air just as unreal and just as menacing as the awful stinging jellyfish below the pier at Southend. But Gladys warmed to the memory of how she would gather younger sister Violet, baby brother Lawrence, and all the other children playing around the neighborhood. After all, the dads and mums were working. Then she would hammer on the piano and sing hymns at the top of her lungs. What child could resist joining such wild, undisciplined frolic? If the distance thundered with bombs from zeppelins, the children never heard it. And all the children would still be flushed with joy long after the zeppelins disappeared.

But Gladys put her sweet memories of Edmonton on hold. Halfway across Siberia, a man in a business suit entered her compartment. He bowed slightly. He was certainly not a typical Russian. "Madam, the conductor asked me to speak to you. Your ticket is to the city of Harbin in Manchuria. The train no longer goes on to Harbin."

"Yes, sir. Thank you so much for informing me." Gladys nodded politely, but her heart jumped.

Was she going to be stopped? What would happen? Was the fighting still going on between the Russians and the warlord Chang Hsueh-liang? Well, in any event she would just stay on the train, no matter what. This wasn't her war.

One by one, as the train continued on its journey, the other civilians got off at their stops, each stop more mountainous than the one before. Only soldiers got on the train now. Soon Gladys seemed not just the only woman aboard but the only civilian too. The soldiers were crude, but watched her in amusement as she periodically opened her suitcase to retrieve a cracker or a cookie. Hot bouillon from her tiny alcohol stove brought real envy to their eyes. But they had their own rations and she didn't dare run out of food before she reached China. And these cold, forbidding mountains they were passing through now frightened her very much.

At the station called Chita, a crewman on the train came into her compartment. "Must leave now. . ."

"Certainly not!" she snapped.

He shrugged and left. The train continued on.

Finally in the night it stopped. Voices erupted everywhere, a real hubbub of activity. Soldiers were tramping up and down the corridor. Doors were slamming. The soldiers in her compartment left so abruptly they didn't bother to close the outside door. Gladys closed it. Then the train was silent. Nothing. It was eerie, uncanny. All that silence in the train, after days of constant clamor.

Gladys tiptoed out into the corridor. In every direction the train was dark. She had the unmistakable feeling she was now really alone. She went back into her compartment and opened the outside door. Pop, pop, pop went the night air.

"Firecrackers?" she mulled as she listened hard. Then the reality hit her. This wasn't one of the footman's tiresome jokes about Chinese firecrackers. What a fool she was. "Those sharp pops are gunfire!"

She ventured out onto the platform. In the distance, presumably on the platform, was a fire. She would investigate. But she dared not leave her belongings. So, wrapped in the fur, she lugged her two bags down the platform toward the fire. There, indeed by a fire on the platform, were four of the train's crewmen, including the one who had asked her in Chita to leave the train.

He shook his head. "See. Train stop here." He wasn't gloating. He was upset. "Go back Chita."

"I was sold a ticket to Dairen on the China Sea," she told him emphatically, "and I expect to be taken there whether your train is running or not."

He shrugged and offered her a cup of coffee, then inundated her with broken English. After much gesticulating, the man convinced Gladys the train would stay there until it was needed to take wounded Russian soldiers back to Chita and beyond. Well, Gladys told him, she would wait and go back too.

"No, it could take many weeks!" he told her. "Soldiers are very dangerous to girl alone!" Besides that, if she waited very long, the man explained in increasing exasperation, the snow would hide the train tracks and she would be hopelessly lost. He shook his fist now. She had no choice but to walk back to Chita. Right away!

"Right away. . ." she muttered and lugged her bags off into the night.

Gladys could scarcely believe the turn of events. In the dead of the Russian winter she was actually trudging through mountain country back to Chita, confined to the shallow snow between the rails. It forced her to stumble over the gapped wooden ties that the rails were spiked into. But she couldn't walk in the deep snow outside the rails. After a while the fire back on the platform was no longer visible. The night was black. Once she was startled to realize she was walking through a tunnel. She fought the silly fear that a train might be coming. She remembered Sir Francis quoting Lord Byron in one of his books:

The scene was savage, but the scene was new;
This made the ceaseless toil of travel sweet,
Beat back keen winter's blast,
And welcomed summer's heat.

Well, she could certainly use some help to beat back winter's blast. Though the sentiment bolstered her, it was not enough. Byron's poetry may have helped Sir Francis crawl down the icy precipice at Mustagh Pass, but her courage came from God. She had only to ask.

"Oh, God Almighty, give me courage," she prayed.

Courage came to drive away her increasing dread. Finally, in one small tunnel, she actually stopped and lit her alcohol stove. The tunnel was the closest thing to shelter she would find. She drank a cup of instant coffee and slowly munched two crackers. That would have to do.

Fatigue overwhelmed her. Wrapped in the fur, she lay under her luggage tented into a crude hut. She was too tired to appreciate what distant barking might mean in the Siberian wilderness. Dogs? Out here? And when she awoke the terrifying danger that lurked behind that barking had vanished in the clean dawn light.

"Praise God for a nice calm day," she said, getting up stiffly. "Coffee and crackers and I'm off to Chita."

All day long she trudged along the mountainous, winding track, snow and great pines in all directions. There was a winter crispness in the air that invigorated her. But that vigor would turn all too easily into a cold weariness, at times a hopelessness. She must reach Chita before nightfall. She couldn't take another Siberian night.

In the dimming evening light, she saw distant dots of light shining like gold. By the time the sky was black she had reached the train platform in Chita. She was too tired to think straight. She saw Russians sitting along the platform, virtually camped on their luggage. She did the same thing. Imagine sleeping outside in the Siberian winter again, she thought as she drifted to sleep.

"Nyet! Nyet! Nyet!" boomed a voice.

Gladys awoke groggily. She peered out of her fur. It was morning. Men were gathered around her. Apparently the railway officials had discovered her. They chattered indecipherably. As strange as Russia was to her, she must have seemed stranger yet to the Russians.

She couldn't let this opportunity escape. "I was sold a ticket to Dairen on the China Sea," she said, emphatically pointing down the track to the southeast. "I expect to be taken there whether your train is running or not. A bus will do just as well."

Later soldiers came to escort her inside the station. They pushed her into a small room. As she insisted they get her going toward China without further delay, they slammed the door in her face. She heard the door lock. She was in the room hour after hour. At one point an official entered to talk to her, but again she understood not one word. He finally shrugged and left, but he made sure he locked her in again.

She spent the night there. But with her tiny stove and a supply of food she was much better off inside the station.

She could scarcely imagine what was to be done with her. But she was certain they were obligated to get her—a British citizen—to her destination.

"Happy morning!" boomed a voice in rough English the next morning.

Now she was questioned by an official she could half-way comprehend. But he couldn't seem to understand at all why she did not want to stay in Russia and work in their great new society. She brushed off this talk and insisted on being allowed to reach the destination she paid for. She repeated "I am a British citizen" until he seemed sickened by it. Reluctantly he finally handed her paperwork and more tickets. She would be put back on a train, he grumbled.

"Am I to understood I will continue on a spur track that somehow will bypass the fighting near the Manchurian border?" she asked.

He shrugged. His job was over.

So she continued on some spur line, periodically pulled off the train at stops to be harassed by officials. Many times she pointed at pictures in her Bible to try to make her points understood, but then she began to try a new tactic. Now she pulled out the photo of her brother Lawrence in his military uniform. As a drummer in the British Army he seemed as grand as Napoleon himself. This tactic got miraculous results. "Why take a chance?" their eyes seemed to say. "Get on with you!"

And although the Russian alphabet was indecipherable to her and she did not know Siberian geography anyway she became convinced the train route was somehow bypassing Manchuria. It was days and much harassment later that she heard a stop announced that she did recognize.

"Vladivostok!" yelled the train official.

"Oh, praise God," murmured Gladys. Vladivostok was a port not on the China Sea but much farther north on the Sea of Japan. At least, though, she was headed in the right direction.

Danger had become almost comic for her, because the officials seemed so half-hearted. But that changed in Vladivostok, where she stayed at the Intourist Hotel, a government-run hotel for tourists only. Gladys was no longer threatened by petty officials with no real stomach for their dirty work. Now she dealt with an unctuous, but professional, Russian bureaucrat. He was a real Communist. And his questions in English were bold.

"Why don't you wish to stay here and work for our great Communist society?" asked the man in suit and tie. "Why go waste your life on that bunch of yellow barbarians to the south? You are white, like me. You are civilized, like me. We can use bright people like you."

"I don't like it here," she answered bluntly. "I wish to take the steamer to Tientsin."

"A steamer to Tientsin? In China? There is no steamer from here to Tientsin. Have you operated machines before?"

"No, and I don't intend to."

Gladys abruptly left the man. She needed time to think. What was she going to do? She noticed a young woman she had seen before—more than once. It almost seemed the woman was following her. Suddenly in the hotel foyer the young woman motioned her to follow her into a corridor. The woman made certain no one else followed. Her eyes looked haunted. She should have been pretty but her face was stony from pure desperation.

43

"Do you know you were just talking to the secret police?" asked the woman breathlessly. "You are in great danger."

"What should I do?"

"You must get out of Vladivostok right away."

"The man with the secret police took my passport. He said they had to process it."

"Get it back, no matter what you have to do. A man will come to your room very late tonight. Go with him."

"Why are you doing this for me?"

"So you don't trust me? I don't blame you. But the vultures are gathering. You must act quickly. If you stay here much longer you will never leave Russia."

Abruptly the woman left. Gladys returned to the secret police to demand her passport. He said he would come to her room later to return it. Later that evening he did. But the man with the secret police wanted something from Gladys first.

"How dare you?" she snapped. "I'm a British citizen."

"Get on the bed."

"God, protect me!" she screamed. "God, protect me!"

The man seemed to boil with anger and doubt. Should he force himself on her? Or leave? It seemed to Gladys that no matter how fearsome the Communist might be, he lived in fear of someone more terrible than himself. Finally the man swore at her angrily and threw the passport at her. He slammed the door as he left. Gladys quickly bolted it. She picked up her passport.

"Praise God. It really is my passport. But what's this? 'Missionary' has been changed to 'Machinist'! So that is what they are planning to do. They will send me to some work camp as a machinist and lie that I volunteered."

Her head was swimming from intrigue. Surely it was only God's protection that got her through so many encounters with such terrible people as these Communists. For now she was sure the evil she was seeing in Russia was not in the Russians but in Communism.

Very late that night a man came to her room. He motioned her to come with him. Was this another wrinkle on some convoluted scheme to spirit her away to a work camp? But what choice did she have? Silently she prayed for Jesus to help her. Then she took her luggage and followed him into the icy night. Stumbling along black streets Gladys smelled the sea, and eventually they came to the docks. The stony-faced young woman appeared.

"So there you are!" exclaimed Gladys, amazed at how much she appreciated the familiarity of that haunted face.

"You will find a Japanese freighter over there. Beg your way on no matter what you have to do. You must leave Russia tonight!"

There it was again: "No matter what you have to do." Surely that was what this poor haunted woman had to do everyday herself to survive. "Why are you taking such a risk for me?" asked Gladys.

"Not all Russians are bad."

"If only I had something to give you. I have so little. Here, take my gloves. And I have some extra stockings."

The woman's eyes glistened with tears. She swallowed hard and took the gloves and stockings. She was thankful but very ashamed of herself and her seedy country. "Hurry. Leave," she said. Abruptly she was gone into the darkness.

Gladys scurried to a hut that guarded the gangplank of

the Japanese freighter. A window glowed with light. She burst inside, startling a man in a seaman's uniform. He sat at a desk littered with papers.

"I must speak to the captain of that Japanese ship!" said Gladys, praying that he would understand enough to take her to the captain.

"Who are you?" he said in perfect English.

"I'm a British citizen. I must get out of Russia on that ship."

"I see," he sighed knowledgeably. "Show me your passport."

"Here it is."

He examined it briefly. "Do you have money?"

"No," she lied, afraid that the seaman would take what little money she had. Then she would have nothing to give the captain.

He handed her the passport and shook his head. "You have no money, but you still want to see the captain so you can get on the ship."

"If you will just take me to the captain I can explain everything to him."

"I am the captain," he said, with no pleasure.

Captain! And she had just told this man she had no money.

five

"No money, no money," muttered the man who said he was captain of the Japanese freighter.

She prayed. Then she begged, "I must leave Russia, captain. The Russian secret police are going to send me to a work camp—or worse."

"A British citizen in great trouble?" he mulled. "Well, no one is a greater friend of the British than a citizen of Japan like myself. All you have to do is sign some papers for me. Then I'll have one of the crewmen take you to a room."

"Praise God for your kindness," she said.

"Praise Japan," he snapped.

Six hours later the freighter was out on the dawn-tinted sea. Gladys had to force herself to look back at Vladivostok, now sinking below the horizon like unwanted sewage. The captain was also on deck surveying the sea, which spread before them like glass.

"This great sea before you is a marvel of tranquillity,"

he announced with a wave of his hand. "It has almost no tide. It rarely allows a typhoon to enter. Even you English call it the 'Sea of Japan'!"

It was the last time she saw the captain until three days later when the freighter docked at a small port named Tsuruga. He told Gladys she had to remain on board until someone came to her from the British consul. He could have put her ashore at once but Gladys knew now he wanted to enjoy the gratitude of British officialdom for rescuing one of their citizens.

Within hours Gladys was onshore sitting in a restaurant with a very young man from the consul. As polite as he was, he seemed not so much a countryman as just one more in a long line of frustrated, bewildered bureaucrats. Whatever was he going to do with Gladys? British citizens just simply did not get themselves marooned in this port of Tsuruga on the west coast of Japan.

"The captain of the freighter told me to go to Kobe," she said forcefully. "There I can get a ship to China."

"Kobe?" His face lit up. "Why, Kobe is just across the island of Japan—on its east coast. Kobe is no more than a pleasant train ride away. We must get you a ticket straightway!"

He was so eager to remove this possible stain on his promising career that he bought the ticket himself. Gladys soon found herself gazing out the window of her compartment at the Japanese countryside. In the distance were mountains. But the train crossed a plain.

There was no sprawling, savage wilderness here. Unlike Russia, Japan was dense with people and houses, yet immaculate too. Trees were bursting with bright red flowers. Fields were neat, ripe with golden crops—not wheat, a man told her, but rice. The people were pleasant and polite. But Gladys was no fool; she was reminded of the "betters" she had worked for. Perhaps these Japanese, like the English upper-class, were also too shrewd, too disciplined, too well-mannered to show displeasure.

"But I must admit," she murmured to herself, watching throngs of sharply dressed people in a town called Ayabe, "that they certainly do not look belligerent."

Other than their belligerence toward China, Gladys knew very little about the Japanese. Of course she knew that Japan had clashed with Russia in the recent past. In fact Japan beat them and gained Korea. So Japan was a formidable military power.

Japan's lack of respect for China had begun to show in 1915, during the Great World War. They made of China "Twenty-One Demands," one of which was that China would never yield any of their coastal territory to a nation other than Japan. China quickly granted the demands, an admission that they were intimidated.

At the same time Japan was arranging various treaties with powers like America and Britain that assured territorial rights of both Japan and China. Many now felt this inclusion of China was because Japan intended to subdue China. In 1916 Japan demanded of China commercial rights in Inner Mongolia and southern Manchuria. The Chinese appeased them.

Most of what Gladys had read had been about Manchuria, the northeasternmost extension of China. Although Russia skirmished with Manchuria, a fact Gladys had just witnessed firsthand, Japan's designs on Manchuria were unrelenting. Each year China gave Japan more concessions in the affairs of Manchuria, as if it were some kind of border issue between the two countries. Yet the Manchus who ruled all of China for 250 years prior to 1911 were Manchurians!

"And yet the Japanese seem so polite," said Gladys in wonder as her train finally reached Kobe.

With the help of the Dyers, English missionaries with the Kobe Mission Hall, Gladys arranged her ticket on a steamer to Tientsin. But that was not all. As a guest in the Dyers' house, she luxuriated in a steam bath, then spent three glorious nights in a real bed. Russia seemed very far away now, a memory she didn't dwell on. There were too many horrors that seemed worse now than when they happened. Was she so naive? The "dogs" barking in the Siberian wilderness the night she slept in the tunnel were of course not dogs at all.

"A pack of slavering wolves. . ." she admitted.

What if they had found her? And what of the soldiers on the train? What if the wrong bunch had found her in her compartment, the only woman, the only civilian? And what if the terrible man from the secret police that night in Vladivostok had decided he could do anything to Gladys he wanted? How lucky she had been. Gladys shuddered.

But what secular nonsense was she thinking? Her escape from such terrors was not just luck. God had protected her. His will always prevailed. "Just as Your will must prevail in China," she prayed.

In Kobe, Gladys boarded a steamer that sailed out into the Pacific Ocean. The Pacific was not only immense but savage. This was no tranquil Sea of Japan. But after the ship rounded Japan and steamed up into the great gulf between China and Korea, the waters progressively calmed.

Gladys became more excited with each passing moment. She spent more time on deck squinting at the distant western horizon. Where was China? Where was Tientsin? One day she saw land to the northeast that a seaman said was Darien, the port that had been her original destination on the Siberian railroad. What extra miles had been forced on her! That same day to her west on the horizon materialized a dark blue fringe that as a seafarer she now recognized as distant land. The fringe grew and greened.

"China—at long last!" she gasped, realizing she was just hours away.

Tientsin made the ports of Vladivostok and Tsuruga, even Kobe, look like country villages. Kobe could compete with it for the amount of shipping in the harbor but the city of Tientsin itself was far larger.

Gladys knew Tientsin had been eagerly embraced by the British since the northern part of China—the China that revolved around Beijing—really opened up a corridor for trade in 1860. Before that time the only five ports open for trade with China were much farther south.

So many buildings had been erected by the British that Tientsin actually looked European. It was a bit disconcerting to Gladys. Certainly this was not the quaint China of her dreams. Nevertheless the Chinese people themselves were from her dreams, maybe even from her unconsciousness, maybe even from Providence.

While riding in a rickshaw to the headquarters of a mission society she was startled to remember how disappointed she had been as a teenage girl with her own tiny stature and black hair—back when she still dreamed of becoming an international star of the stage. And here she was now among short, black-haired people. The similarity had never even occurred to her before. It was strange how the past tweaked her with no warning.

Gladys called at the mission society in Tientsin. "Jeannie Lawson said I was to wait here until she sent a guide for me," she told a woman missionary.

"Jeannie Lawson?" gasped the woman. "Oh gracious me, I don't think so. That could take a very long time. You see we would have to get in touch with her. Then she would have to get in touch with us and. . ."

"But. . ."

"You must just go on ahead and find her."

"Find her?"

"Yes, she is a bit of a renegade, you see."

"An elderly missionary woman?"

The woman smiled indulgently. "Jeannie Lawson travels around in the province of Shansi pretty much as she pleases."

The mission society took Gladys in, while they searched for someone dependable she could travel to Shansi with. In the meantime, she explored. She was quick to discover the Great Wall, which she would not see for many days yet, was in itself a real symbol for Chinese history. Walls were everywhere. Walls, walls, walls. Villages and towns were walled. The smaller villages consisted of one main street lined on both sides by walled buildings. So each building was a small fortress in itself. A visitor went in one gate of the village and went out the other. At night the gates were locked. The poorest of the poor lived outside the walls. The missionaries told her villages all over China were built on that plan, a plan that must have gone back through thousands of years of mistrust.

"And the walls are still there," said one missionary pointedly.

Gladys also began to learn about the Chinese language. The remarks of the principal at the China Inland Mission Center at London had long haunted her. She prayed that God would allow her, at nearly thirty, to learn Chinese. It was certainly a peculiar language to any person who spoke English. Words were generally one syllable. Chinese was spoken with very little inflection, with no raising and lowering of volume for emphasis. But Chinese was anything but monotonous because it was a tonal language. Completely alien to any English speaker, the Chinese had words that sounded the same but meant completely different things depending on whether the pitch was constant, rising, falling, rising then falling, or falling then rising! In theory the same sound could mean many different things.

"Don't look so worried, Gladys," said one missionary, "Around here and in Shansi the Mandarin sub-language usually has only four tones. And your Chinese listeners will often figure out your meaning from the context."

Gladys listened willingly to this information about language but her head was spinning. Written Chinese could be understood by educated people all over China. But the actual words for the symbols were so different there were seven main sub-languages called *gwan-has* and within them thousands of dialects called *tu-hwas*.

As an example of how difficult that made unifying China, one only had to realize that the Nationalist Party President Chiang Kai-shek spoke fluently only *Wu,* the sub-language known around Shanghai. He could barely make himself understood to those who spoke Mandarin in the north of China. Nor could he understand them.

"That's one of the reasons Sun Yat-sen called China a 'dish of sand,' " commented one missionary.

"Cheer up, Gladys," commented another. "The Mandarin sub-language you will learn is spoken by two out of three Chinese. That's about three hundred million people!"

That was one consolation. But other facts about languages fell on her like ax blows. Chinese offered few aids to grammar. There was nothing to indicate whether verbs, nouns, and adjectives agreed with each other in number and case; because of that, word order was critical. Whereas in English the subject performed an action, in Chinese the subject was often merely followed by a comment. And because there were no tenses of verbs, the foreigner became quite confused over whether something happened, was happening, or was going to happen! There was no written alphabet; there were instead thousands of symbols: no less than one symbol for each word. Knowing two thousand symbols was the minimum needed to decipher a simple newspaper.

"Don't worry, Gladys. There are probably no newspapers where you will be," said one missionary tactlessly.

Life at the mission society was a double-edged sword. Gladys learned much but was overwhelmed too. She was very pleased when the mission finally made arrangements for her to travel to Shansi with a Chinese businessman.

Mr. Lu, a Christian, wore a dark blue robe and a fedora hat. First the two rode the train. Chinese passenger train cars were not like European train cars, with outside doors to every compartment. Instead there were only two doors, one on each end of the car. So the Chinese thronged against the two doors. Even so, Gladys and Mr. Lu found a seat, though passengers kept entering the car until the floor was packed too. Then travelers started climbing on top of the car. It seemed as if a hundred people chattered and thumped above Gladys.

"Car is very strong," assured Mr. Lu.

"Let us pray that is so," commented Gladys.

As the train gathered speed, she expected someone to tumble off the top and flash by her window at any moment. But nothing happened. A guard maintained order inside the car. If someone wanted off he threatened passengers with his nightstick until a pathway was cleared. And he didn't mind wedging in a new passenger where there seemed no room at all.

The train chugged across a river plain of gold-stubbled paddies. The rice had already been harvested. Mr. Lu explained that the locals also farmed peanuts, beans, and corn. A few cottonwoods and sycamores could be seen near mud-walled villages that hugged the track. Here and there were small, rock-walled cemeteries. On deeply rutted roads two-wheel carts rattled along, pulled by shaggy ponies.

"Blue seems to be everyone's favorite color in China," commented Gladys.

"It is the cheapest dye for clothes," offered Mr. Lu. "From a root found all over China."

"Oh."

At stations, men would rush to her window and try to sell her pink and white lotus blossoms. She had no money to spare for anything but transportation and sustenance.

Just before one nightfall, she saw the great towers and walls of Beijing rise ahead. Now here was a city that could occupy a dozen lifetimes. Within the city was the palatial complex of the old emperors. Gladys would get little more than a glimpse. Outside Beijing she saw the Great Wall of China itself. Sir Francis's description she had memorized from *The Heart of a Continent* became reality:

> *all along these heights, as far as the eyes*
> *could see, ran this wonderful wall, going down*
> *the side of one hill, up the next, over its summit*
> *and down the other side again. . .thirty or forty*
> *feet high, of solid stone, and fifteen feet or so*
> *thick. . .with towers every few hundred feet. . . .*

The Great Wall ran for fifteen hundred miles east to west, informed Mr. Lu. Its purpose, to keep out invaders from the north, had long since been defeated. Mr. Lu added that the wall had been very logically placed just at the northern limit of decent farming country.

"Land north of the Great Wall is considered virtual desert," he said with a smile.

Three days later the railway track ran out. From there they rode busses to the south. Often now they spent the night at inns. Inns were no surprise to Gladys. She had read about them in Sir Francis's travels. The inns of course were always walled and their entrance gate to the one main street closed up at night.

In the open-aired central yard of the inn were busses and carts. Along one wall were stalls for horses and mules. On the other side the guests were herded into one or more rooms. They were fed bowls of steaming rice and vegetables. Onions, bamboo sprouts, water chestnuts, yams, cabbage, and carrots were flavored with garlic, anise, and ginger. Gladys had heard of delicacies like sugared lotus seeds, bird's nest-soup, and limed eggs, but nothing like that was served at an inn she could afford. No form of meat made the menu where she stayed either. Nor were bread products known in these rice-eating areas, she learned from Mr. Lu.

Occasionally before the gate was locked, villagers would flock into the inn to look at Gladys. Mr. Lu would then try to shoo them away. "What are they saying?" Gladys would ask. But Mr. Lu seemed too embarrassed to translate. Gladys was almost glad then that she could not understand their comments. But one greeting was becoming familiar to her.

"Chi-la fan ma?" asked some who met her.

Mr. Lu explained it literally meant "Have you eaten?," but it was intended to be a polite greeting. Gladys guessed the expression stemmed from the Chinese obsession with food, because they rarely had enough. Overweight Chinese were not to be seen. The proper response to the polite greeting was "Yes, I have eaten," in Chinese, "Chi-la."

Before retiring, the guests visited the toilet. Their toilets were a shock to Gladys. They were narrow trenches near the far end of the courtyard, usually shielded only by a flimsy fence of cornstalks. Mr. Lu said their contents were guarded zealously too. The contents were used to fertilize the small gardens, a fact which explained a pervasive and very offensive smell to Gladys. No one else seemed to notice.

The guests slept on a *kang*. This was a raised mud or

brick platform under which hot air was billowed from a stove maintained in the kitchen. In theory the kang was warm. All Gladys knew was that it was very hard, in spite of a mat that covered it. Some of the travelers used bricks for pillows, if one could call such a hard thing a pillow! Some had a special "ear pillow," a small stuffed cushion with a space conveniently hollowed out for the ear.

Mr. Lu told Gladys, "Everyone in the colder regions of China sleep on kangs."

Often the inn had only one enormous room for guests. Then there was no privacy at all. Everyone slept on a communal kang. Usually no one undressed, but if one wanted to undress he did so under the blankets. Mr. Lu told Gladys it was customary to undress under the covers, even in the privacy of a home. And the next morning the Chinese dressed under the covers as well.

Gladys was quick to notice that everyone turned their shoes over and shook them before putting them on again in the morning. For once, Mr. Lu could not think of the English words to explain the horror of not shaking the shoes. So Gladys shook her shoes. One morning something dropped out a man's shoe. It tried to skitter away. The man swatted it with his shoe.

"Scorpion," gulped Gladys.

Not every stop was a village with one main street. They stayed on the outskirts of several sprawling populaces, large cities by anyone's standards. And she had to remind herself that China had over four hundred million people. Britain had one-tenth as many.

The two continued on to the south by bus, day after draining day. They were flanked by the heights of the

Shansi province. This high country of Shansi was in a sense mountainous, explained Mr. Lu, but some said it was really a high plateau riddled by very deep canyons. He shrugged as if to say "what difference does it make?"

About the only change in the long trip that Gladys noticed was the disappearance of bowls of rice at the inns and the appearance of bowls of thick doughy noodles.

One month after leaving Tientsin, their route finally veered into the foothills and Gladys arrived in Tsechow. Here Gladys felt she was in ancient China. Tsechow was an important trading center. Trucks as well as great ambling, loose-lipped camels brought tobacco, silks, and other fabrics from the direction Gladys had just come herself, then headed back that same route toward Beijing with coal, ironware, and cotton. The gracious Mr. Lu took her to the doorstep of the China Inland Mission. Gladys barely had time to thank him before she was peppered with conversation from an elderly Mrs. Smith, who ran the mission. Admittedly seventy years old, she had survived her missionary husband by many years. Of course, Gladys already knew elderly women were common at the missions in China. In fact, Mrs. Smith was helped by another elderly woman, trained as a nurse. But where was Jeannie Lawson?

"Oh, Jeannie," said Mrs. Smith, smiling, "is off in the mountains. Yangcheng, we heard."

"Is it far?"

"One day to Chowtsun, another day to Yangcheng."

"Bus?"

"Dear me, no. You'll be finding no busses in the mountains. All transport is by mule on trails as old as civilization. Yangcheng is on an age-old mule trail that runs through the high country from the far north to the south."

That evening Mrs. Smith expounded on her beloved province of Shansi. The Chinese here ate wheat, millet, and barley, not rice. Shansi was almost the cradle of Chinese civilization, she said. Hidden within the mountains to the west was the fertile valley of the Fen river that brought its water from the north to the south. The area was virtually the center of China until the Tang dynasty.

"And when was that?" asked Gladys uncertainly.

"About 600 A. D. Practically yesterday. The Fen Valley has been farmed for four thousand years."

"China certainly changes one's perspective," gasped Gladys. "How long have you lived here?"

"Oh, for almost fifty years."

"Fifty years! You must have been among the very first missionaries."

"Yes, my husband was one of the group some people call the Cambridge Seven."

"The Cambridge Seven! Then you must be Mrs. Stanley Smith!"

"Oh dear, you mustn't carry on so."

Gladys went to bed numb. She had been talking to a woman almost legendary in mission circles. The Cambridge Seven had captivated the British with their commitment to the China Inland Mission. They were all from Cambridge University, all from the English upper class. Several were famous sports stars as well. C. T. Studd was famous for cricket. Huge, raw-boned Stanley Smith had been the captain of Cambridge's eight-man rowing crew. Smith had also been deemed the best preacher of the Cambridge Seven.

Of course Gladys had seen celebrated people before.

After all, she had worked in Belgrave Square. Still, it was glorious to be among God's servants. And Mrs. Smith even treated her, Gladys the parlor maid, as an equal!

"Surely this is a great gift to me from God," reflected Gladys. "Hallelujah!"

The next morning Mrs. Smith sent word for a mule *shanza*. She also advised Gladys that her western clothes were no longer appropriate. For one thing, it was never advisable in the mountains to advertise one was a foreigner. For another thing, Gladys's dress, which Gladys considered very modest, showed too much of her neck. She had to have a high collar of some kind. Anything less was considered very immoral. Soon Gladys was attired in standard Chinese wear: high-collared blue jacket and blue trousers. She had also learned Chinese did not wear underwear. They simply added layer after layer of the same style of clothing as the weather demanded. Naturally each successive layer had to be a larger size.

"You will know a 'four-layer' day up in Yangcheng sooner or later," advised Mrs. Smith. "And the cloth will be quilted and padded with cotton besides."

That was probably only an inkling of unknowns yet to come, reflected Gladys.

And when the muleteer and his assistant arrived outside the mission with the mule shanza it certainly was nothing like she imagined.

six

No, the mule shanza awaiting Gladys outside the mission house was certainly nothing like she had imagined. Lying on the ground were two poles about eight feet long and separated by two three-foot crossbars. Between the two long poles and the crossbars was a network of interlaced rope. On this network the muleteer placed Gladys's two bags, one feathery light now, since she had consumed almost all of the food she had brought from England. Then over the rope network the muleteer placed a *bei-tao,* or mattress. Matting was arched to form a canopy. The muleteer's assistant appeared with a saddled mule.

"You best get in the shanza," said Mrs. Smith.

Gladys crawled in and sat under the canopy. She said, "But shouldn't the mule. . ."

Suddenly the front end of the crossbars shot up in the air so violently Gladys thought she was going to be launched into space. The muleteer and his assistant dropped the front ends of the crossbars into grooves on the saddle. Barely hanging on, Gladys thought she heard another mule being brought up behind her. Suddenly the rear end of the crossbars rose in space and then plopped down. Gladys didn't have to look to know the crossbars had settled into grooves on the second mule's saddle.

"Muleteers can be a bit rough at times," commented Mrs. Smith, smothering a smile. Suddenly the whole contraption lurched forward. "Nor does time wait for a muleteer," shouted Mrs. Smith with glee. " 'Bye, Gladys."

Gladys had never been in an earthquake but she was sure it could not have been much worse than this wild ride in a shanza. But soon the ride smoothed out as the strides of two mules fell into unison. Gladys even became complacent as the shanza proceeded along terrain no worse than the hills of England. This went on for several miles but then as her feet began to elevate she realized the mules were clopping up a rocky trail. She peered out from under the canopy. Still not too bad. But an hour later she began to hold her breath every time she looked out. There seemed not enough room to leave the shanza without stepping into space and falling hundreds of feet down a vertical cliff.

"God will protect me," she prayed.

The mountains were starkly bare except occasionally where some enterprising Chinese had terraced a plot to farm his corn or millet or wheat.

By nightfall they reached Chowtsun, a small walled village perched on the side of the mountain. The mule shanza was whisked into an inn. By now Gladys knew exactly what to expect in an inn. But some of these people, rather than being curious, screeched and fled in terror. After that reaction, she tried to remain very unnoticed. For the first time in China she was helpless to communicate with anyone. Their language was unintelligible to her as the chittering of birds.

"But just as delightful," she told herself.

The next day her muscles were very sore from the rolling and pitching of the mule shanza but she was elated. At long last her journey was almost over. And the sight that greeted her after one bend in the trail was more wonderful than anything she had ever imagined—and she had imagined much.

Beyond them the mountain was not bare, but terraced with crops and even greened here and there with trees. Yangcheng itself was an ancient fairy tale told to her for the first time. Of course it clung to the south side of a mountain, to bathe itself in the sun. Its soft tan walls grew out of the mountainside like an eagle's nest. Tiled roofs rose tantalizingly above the walls. The stacked roofs with their curled-up eaves seemed magical.

"At long last I am here."

One significance of the walls of the enchanted village of Yangcheng was not lost on Gladys. She seemed right in the midst of one of her favorite Bible stories, that of Nehemiah. Yes, Nehemiah the restorer of the walls of Jerusalem, the restorer of the gates of Jerusalem. What would Gladys restore in this magical land?

But Gladys never entered the walls of Yangcheng. Near the East Gate the muleteer led the shanza off to a cluster of dwellings—the abodes of the poor—hugging the mountainside below the walls of the village. Suddenly they stopped.

Gladys peered from under her canopy. They were in front of a large walled building with a front door hanging askew on one hinge. "Could this be. . ."

Whomp!

Gladys felt as if her brain was rattling around inside her head. The muleteer and his assistant had loosed the rear ends of the poles and the shanza had dropped like a rock to the ground. Gladys was going to complain to the men as they walked past her, then realized the front ends would soon be falling too. She scrambled out of the shanza.

A woman as tiny as Gladys, dressed in blue robe and pants, faced her with her hands on her hips. The woman had snow white hair. Fierce sky blue eyes were not softened by small round "granny" spectacles.

"Chi-la fan ma?" she asked.

"Oh, have I eaten?" blurted Gladys. "Well yes, *chi-la,* thank you very much for asking, but no, I haven't really eaten. I'm starved. Well, what I mean to say is. . ."

"English?" interrupted the woman. "Who would you be then?"

"Why, I'm Gladys Aylward. Are you Jeannie Lawson?"

"Well, of all the. . ." The woman brushed her question off as ridiculous. "You'll be coming in then," she said and scurried inside the building.

Gladys passed through the doorway and entered the courtyard. The building was two-storied, spacious and sturdy but very littered. Jeannie Lawson pointed at this pile of rubbish and at that broken door, chattering all the while as if Gladys had known her for a lifetime. Her accent was very thick. Gladys knew it was Scottish at one time. But this strangely accented English had been shaped by fifty years in China. Sometimes Gladys strained almost in agony to understand what Jeannie Lawson said, only to realize she was speaking Chinese.

"So this is your mission house," mused Gladys during one of Jeannie Lawson's few pauses.

"Maybe and maybe not," replied Jeannie Lawson stubbornly. "I've just rented it. I could only afford it because the locals think it's haunted. I know you're burning up with curiosity to know what the rent is. . ."

"Why, no."

"Less than one pound sterling a year! There, now you know. Are you satisfied? Anyway, now that you're here we'll have it cleaned up in no time."

"Then it will be a mission house."

"Maybe and maybe not."

Gladys heard a commotion outside and wandered over to the only door that opened to the street. A ball of mud struck her shoulder and she heard a child scream *"Lao-yang-kwei! lao-yang-kwei!"* and scuffle off. She turned to Jeannie Lawson.

"Lao-yang-kwei. They called you a foreign devil," sighed Jeannie Lawson as if it happened a hundred times a day. Gladys had read in Sir Francis's travels that the Chinese could be very hostile to strangers, but she had not wanted to believe it was true as a generality. But perhaps it was. *"Mu yu fadze,"* said Jeannie Lawson. She seemed to startle herself by speaking Chinese, so she quickly translated, "It can't be helped." She sighed again. "They are even more frightened of me because of my white hair. Very few Chinese have white hair. Be thankful those urchins couldn't find any stones."

"Are they all like that?" asked Gladys uneasily.

"Not all." She clapped her hands and screamed, "Yang!"

An elderly Chinese man appeared out of a room Gladys had not examined yet. "This is Yang, my. . .our cook," she explained. "Yang is not afraid of foreign devils." She fired some Chinese at Yang. Yang laughed.

Jeannie showed Gladys into the only room besides their kitchen that she had managed to clean. In the room she had a table and two chairs. On the wall that the room shared with the kitchen was a kang with its bedding. Boxes were stacked near the opposite wall. A while later Yang returned with a bowl of steamed vegetables and doughy noodles. It was for Gladys. She felt much better after that.

"Thank You, Lord," she prayed that night. "I can't wait to get started."

If there was one thing Gladys was an expert at it was cleaning. Even Jeannie, who seemed impressed by almost nothing, paused once in a while with her hands on her hips as if to marvel at Gladys. Because Gladys transformed the building. Basically there were several smaller rooms but most importantly there were three very large rooms with kangs that would make excellent dormitories. Yang was able to help Gladys repair the doors. Yes, these broken-down doors were her "Nehemiah's gates" to restore. So Gladys never doubted for a moment the building would make a most excellent mission house.

Of course getting the Chinese of Yangcheng to enter the building was another problem. Her few excursions outside were met by the Chinese with blatant contempt. The only thing that kept them from attacking her, according to Jeannie, was their fear of the local Mandarin who apparently had decreed that there was to be no violence done on foreigners.

But soon Gladys had the building ready for more occupants. "When are we going to open our mission house?" she asked.

"I'm still thinking on it."

Jeannie was cantankerous to be sure. And sometimes she did seem teetering on the edge of sanity. But how could Gladys know what memories might haunt the old missionary? So Gladys waited.

One day she was watching one mule train after another mule train plod into the East Gate of Yangcheng. Mule train after mule train plodded out of the gate going the other direction.

A mule train was a sight. Even a child of the city like Gladys knew the mule resulted from mating a male donkey with a female horse. The result was a beast as placid and durable as a donkey but as large and powerful as a horse. In the trains the mules were loaded down with coal and cotton and metal goods. Because mules would taint grain with their smell, the train also consisted of men walking on foot, laden with sacks of wheat, millet, and corn. A train could consist of six to ten mules and twice that many men. Jeannie said these men were like sailors. A complete circuit of the trade route took about three months. Many of these men had several wives along the route. It struck Gladys that the muleteers and their many helpers were just about the only ones who tied the entire province together.

"You know," Gladys said to Jeannie, "if you could convert a muleteer he could carry the gospel all over Shansi."

"How did you figure that out!" Jeannie looked as if Gladys had slapped her.

"Whatever do you mean?"

"I mean you've stolen my idea."

"But. . ."

"We're going to open an inn. We'll regale the muleteers with stories of the gospel. They will carry those stories all over Shansi. Oh, why didn't I tell you sooner? Now you'll think it was your idea."

"But I don't care. . ."

"Don't you dare suggest a name for the inn. Don't even think it! *I'm* going to name it."

Now Gladys was sure Jeannie suffered from some disease of old age. She had worked among too many people too long not to recognize it. Yes, it was some form of senility, but a more disagreeable form. The afflicted was unpredictably belligerent. The worst afflicted victims raged. Yes, Gladys had seen it before. It never got better. This suspected illness became a great worry to her. What if something happened to Jeannie? How in the world would Gladys ever manage alone in Yangcheng? After all, people ran from her, spat at her, threw mud at her. Gladys was a foreign devil. . .

"Well, aren't you ever going to ask me?" snapped Jeannie angrily.

"Ask you what?"

"The name for our inn, as if you didn't know what I meant."

"I thought you. . ."

"The Inn of Eight Happinesses. You see I thought of it first."

"Of course you did. However did you think of such a clever name?"

"Eight is a very lucky number in China." Jeannie beamed. "The word for 'eight' sounds like the word for 'prosperity.' Many of their legends use the number 'eight.' The Eight Immortals. The Eight Diagrams. The Eight Treasures. The Eight Princes."

"I never would have thought of such a clever name."

"I know. And I know you're burning with curiosity about the eight happinesses."

"Well, I suppose they could be something like the fruits of the. . ."

"Devotion, virtue, gentleness, tolerance, loyalty, truth, beauty and most of all, love!" screamed Jeannie.

"Of course."

Thus their inn was born. But one thing was lacking: customers. They tried to spread the word among the villagers and the passing muleteers. Yang tried to spread the word too but still no one came. Jeannie and Gladys took turns standing at their door and screaming *Mu yo beatcha! Mu yo goodso! How, how, how. Lai! Lai! Lai!"* which meant "We have no bedbugs. We have no fleas! Good, good, good. Come! Come! Come!" The plea seemed to make the mules break into a trot—away from their inn. Nothing seemed to draw the mules or muleteers into the inn.

Gladys could see Jeannie was thinking very hard. One morning the old lady appeared very perky.

"Are the dormitories properly cleaned?" asked Jeannie.

How tempted Gladys was to say sarcastically they were just as clean as the day before and the day before that and the day before that. But she couldn't risk riling Jeannie. "Yes, they are properly clean."

"Do we have plenty of hay for the mules?"

"Yes, I checked the fodder only this morning," replied Gladys wearily.

"Then I'll get Yang to prepare plenty of good food. And you will bring in our first mule train."

"What? You know that refrain we yell at every passing train doesn't work."

"I've thought it through and through. These trains will have to be led in by force."

"Force!"

"Just make sure the muleteer appears to searching for an inn. Yang says it's unethical to steal another inn's regular customer."

Gladys couldn't believe such a bizarre thing was happening to her, but it was she who had to watch for the first muleteer that day who appeared to be gawking about for an inn. Then she dashed out in front of his mule train to lunge at the lead mule and grab one of the poor beast's huge ears. How she scuffled and fought the frightened animal to get it into the inn. The lead muleteer screamed at her all the while. Once the mules in the train smelled the hay and water though, they clomped to the stalls to eat and drink. After that the innkeepers had to deal with the still fuming lead muleteer. The other muleteer and his helpers were frozen in fear at the foreign devils.

"Chi-la fan ma?" asked Yang, just at the right time.

Yang motioned the muleteer to the room where they were to eat and whisked by him with the most appetizing food he had ever prepared. Finally the muleteer, almost in tears he was so frustrated, studied his contented mules. He seemed to admit to himself he wouldn't be able to budge the mules for many hours, and with a shrug trudged inside the room where they ate.

They learned his name was Hsi-Lien. His wife and

family lived in Tsechow. Slowly his helpers drifted in too. Jeannie and Gladys treated the guests like royalty. Gladys of course knew every nuance of making people feel comfortable. How she pampered the guests. It was Yang who told stories to their first guests. All Gladys knew at the time was that his story made Jeannie's eyes open wide with concern. It was the next day that Jeannie repeated to Gladys Yang's version of how Noah filled the ark with animals and sailed safely to the inn at Bethlehem.

"Still our own inn is now really born," Gladys rationalized.

Even winter did not stop the activity. Icicles hung everywhere, sparkling like sculptured glass. The walls of Yangcheng caught the blowing snow and piled it into great drifts. The snow swallowed sounds. All inside and outside the city was white and frigid and silent. But still the mules came clomping to Yangcheng on the trails, their breath steaming the frigid air, their great sweating bodies fogging the atmosphere.

The three in the inn worked very hard. And the news of their special hospitality spread. Soon they had half a dozen mule trains staying at the inn every night. The inn teemed with life now. In the stalls were usually forty to fifty mules. The three dormitories were bursting with as many as one hundred muleteers and helpers.

The guests were now enough at ease that Jeannie could tell the stories in the evening. But the inventive Yang was promised he could tell one every week or so. He was most anxious to continue his tale of how Noah fed the five thousand in Nazareth. With Jeannie's help Gladys began to memorize Bible stories in Chinese. She was determined to master the language so she could spread the gospel too.

The success of the inn made things easier for the two women in Yangcheng too. Now when her work was done Gladys could venture inside the walled city to see the sights and practice the language. But one day at the main square a large crowd had gathered.

"What is the excitement all about?" she asked a Chinese woman, upset with herself that she still could not speak Chinese well enough to be understood.

The crowd surrounded a man on his knees. His head was bent forward. A soldier stood over him. Suddenly a huge blade glistened in the sun like lightning. It fell. Red fluid spurted into the air like a pulsing fountain. A head rolled in the street. Gladys screamed. Surely her eyes were lying. She turned—a thousand banshees screaming in her head—and stumbled back to the inn. It was a good while before she could speak of the abomination.

"It is the law here for particular crimes," said Jeannie Lawson.

"But it was horrible."

"I'm sure," said Jeannie coldly, "that the man was tried at the *yamen*."

Gladys knew by now the yamen was like a city hall. The local Mandarin ruled there with absolute authority. In addition to Yangcheng their particular Mandarin presided over several other mountain communities.

"But it was so barbaric," muttered Gladys.

"More barbaric than a hanging, more barbaric than a firing squad?"

"But. . ."

"But nothing. The man was not murdered but executed for some crime. He may have been a bandit or a murderer.

73

His body will thrown off the mountainside. His head will be displayed on the city wall."

"How dreadful!"

"You want them to show more mercy, but we can only change their behavior by patiently doing what we are doing. It will be by the love of Christ that they become more merciful, not by our own emotional desires."

"It was so ghastly, so violent. . ."

"Yes, violent people they can be," muttered Jeannie.

And for the first time Jeannie told Gladys of the Boxer Rebellion. It seemed only yesterday to her, those bloody months of 1900 that the organization of murderous thugs called the Boxers supposedly rebelled. After all, Jeannie had been in the province of Shansi almost from the first day it opened up to missionaries in 1876.

"In 1899 we had an inkling something was horribly wrong," said Jeannie. "A missionary named Brooks was hacked to death out in the wilds. Then there was a change in the provincial government. Our province is governed from the city of Taiyuan, about two hundred miles north of us by mule. To get Yu Hsien, a rabid hater of Europeans farther away from the trading ports, the empress sent him to govern Shansi."

Gladys, now sensing Jeannie was very troubled by her memories and might become too riled, said, "Perhaps you had best not. . ."

"The truth will set us free. Almost as soon as Yu Hsien got to Taiyuan the placards started going up all over the province: 'Out with the foreign devils.' But that was mild compared to the crowds that chanted *'Sha! Sha! Sha!'*"

"I'm afraid to ask. . ."

"Kill! Kill! Kill!"

"Oh."

"Well, you can imagine what can happen when the authorities encourage such hatred. We had about 150 Protestant missionaries in Shansi then, about half of them with Hudson Taylor's bunch, the China Inland Mission. But there were quite a few from the Baptist Mission Society, the American Board, and others too. Quite a lot of Catholic priests and nuns were here and there too. In June of 1900 the Chinese empress simply let the Boxers 'rebel.' All adult Christians in the vicinity of Taiyuan—thirty-three Protestants and twelve Catholics—were arrested. Then the executions began. At first the missionaries were murdered by the executioner's traditional ax, but then the killers became too impatient to wait for the ax. So they used their swords. The Boxers killed all forty-five Christians. And out in the other towns and villages of Shansi we didn't even know the wholesale murder of Christians had erupted. . . ."

seven

Jeannie Lawson continued, "Praise God, we Christians out in the province got the terrible news before the local Boxers did."

"But what did you do?" asked Gladys.

"Well, you can imagine we hid everywhere. In caves. In brush along the rivers. In the cemeteries. Anywhere. . ."

Jeannie went on for a long time with her harrowing experiences fleeing the murderers in the Boxer Rebellion. The missionaries were almost caught by the killers a time or two, but through God's grace they escaped death.

"And you lived through all that," said Gladys in awe.

"And so did my husband and our children." Jeannie's eyes were moist. "But the Boxers caught most of the other missionaries in Shansi. Over a hundred missionaries died. Children died too. Who can explain the mysteries of God?" She glared at Gladys. "So you see execution, after legal process, for committing a crime is not so bad after all."

True to Jeannie's word the man's head was displayed

on the wall. Jeannie reminded Gladys the English used to do the very same thing. Many a severed head had been displayed in London. The head of a king or two had been among them. Gladys prayed she would see the day in China when such executions and displays ceased. And God forbid she would ever witness several heads displayed as Jeannie said had happened before. The more she thought about the executions, the less she was impressed by Jeannie's justification.

"In fact, it seems profoundly unchristian."

But perhaps Jeannie had been speaking out of her illness. Who knew when she was normal and when she was not? Jeannie was snippy and combative all the time. Sometimes she seemed a threat to Gladys. Yet other times Gladys felt she might have imagined the signs of mental deterioration. Sometimes what Jeannie said seemed outrageous but in fact it was true; it was an outrage of China. Still, her illness hung over Gladys's head.

"I must go out among the people and learn to survive among them," Gladys advised herself.

She had already experienced a "four-layer" day, as Mrs. Smith in Tsechow had predicted. Snow fell and accumulated on the icy mountainside. And in spite of the frigid conditions, Gladys had shed her leather high-top shoes to adapt to the Chinese footwear.

They scarcely deserved to be called shoes. They were cloth uppers sewn onto tree bark soles. They wore out in two or three weeks. That was why ten or twelve pairs were bought at one time.

There were other differences in Chinese fashion to which Gladys had to accustom herself. For instance, the women did not comb their hair. They pulled it into tight knots on top or in back and plastered it all down with a goo also made from tree bark. The famous pigtail the Chinese men had been forced to wear under the Manchus was still in vogue in this remote village, although Gladys had noticed in the lowlands it was much less common. Facial hair was not seen on any men but the oldest, as if it had become too much of a chore to shave the whiskers or pluck them out. The women shuffled when they walked, and to her disappointment, Gladys discovered their feet, as the western world claimed, were indeed bound, so that the toes curled under.

"All adult women here have their feet contorted into grotesque club feet!" she blurted to Jeannie one day.

"Then praise God your own toes are free," she answered.

When Jeannie felt especially ornery she would wiggle her toes for curious village women, who now approached them boldly. Jeannie told Gladys the gawkers made remarks that the foreign women's feet were about as elegant as an elephant's feet. Because Gladys wore a size three shoe she did see some humor in that. And the gawkers thought their hands just as cloddish, especially their thick stumps of fingers. Gladys looked at her tiny hands and fingers and had to laugh at that too.

Some of their customs were quaint. For example, if two people met on a narrow path the one who stopped first was allowed the right of way. So anticipating such an encounter was second nature to them. Gladys was never able to be the first to stop. Always she had to step off the path and slog into the mud or snowdrift to let the other person pass. Jeannie said that was the custom over all the parts of

China she had seen. Such a universal custom was amazing, because most Chinese did very little traveling. For centuries, in these parts only the muleteers were even remotely like the common people in England who traveled about freely.

"Yes, there are many of the same customs that I have observed everywhere I have gone in China," marveled Jeannie.

Their customs and traditions were quite specific too. Once Gladys observed a woman who refused to sit with another woman, a relative. Why? Because the woman already sitting was the woman's mother-in-law's older brother's wife! Both of them sitting together was unthinkable. Relationships took precedent over age. For example, in large families a niece might very well be older than an aunt. But a twenty-year-old niece must never get familiar with a ten-year-old aunt. She must respectfully call her "Fourth-Younger-Aunt-On-My-Father's-Side"—in the home as well as in public.

And of course there was the fine art of "saving face." Contrary to what westerners thought this meant, a gracious person did everything possible to let the *other* person save face. If for example Yang found out a delivery man had been overcharging him for yams, Yang would inform the man the two foreign women had told him he must cut back on the money he spent on yams. Thus warned, the shrewd man would continue to deliver the same amount of yams but charge Yang less. Or if Yang decided a particular delivery man simply had to be terminated he would pass the word to one of the man's relatives. Soon enough the delivery man would appear one day to tell Yang he couldn't make deliveries to the inn anymore; he was moving on to bigger and better things.

Gladys learned wedding customs too. From the guests' standpoint it was a great occasion for eating. And when the banquet after the ceremony ended, the guests abruptly left, as if to say *"mu yu la,"* "all gone." But for Gladys the highlight was the ceremony. At the groom's house, to the music of fiddles, flutes, and drums, the bride and groom arrived, each on a separate litter. The bride wore an elegant red silk robe and her face was covered by a red scarf. She could not be seen by the groom before the wedding. The groom wore everyday blue clothing, but adorned by a bright red sash. Equality of the two was an illusion. In the ritual that followed, Jeannie told Gladys later, the bride was exhorted to obey her husband. If Gladys had seen the bride's bedroom she would seen chopsticks over the door.

"It's a pun," explained Jeannie. "The pronunciation of the word for chopsticks is almost identical with the pronunciation of the words for 'Quick Son'! In other words, nothing would please the groom more than to have a son just as quickly as possible."

Jeannie said it without emotion. In fifty years she had truly accepted many of the ways of the Chinese. But Gladys had not. Many of the things she learned about marriages disturbed her. First of all, the bride had nothing whatever to say about her choice of a husband. It was all arranged. A very young husband had no say either. But if a man became wealthy, then he could pick and choose his new wives. He could have as many as he could afford. But he never bragged about how many wives he had. No, it was only the number of his sons that he ever boasted about.

If asked "how many children do you have?" a man

would proudly answer, "I have five sons." Daughters were never mentioned at all.

The sooner a man could get started on his flock of sons the better. It was not uncommon for a man of wealth to make sure his son barely in the first stages of puberty took a wife several years older. This gave the boy a nice head start on his own sons, according to Chinese custom. It was obvious love played no part in matchmaking. If love developed between a man and his wife it happened later. But the wife never attained equality.

Even at funerals the man reigned. No expense was spared for the man. Of course a poor man didn't fare much better than his wife. But a funeral for a wealthy man was an elaborate event. Ornate banners and screens were rented to surround the gravesite, which in these steep mountains was a hole in the side of a cliff. A rented cannon was there too, to be fired every hour of the first day to scare away evil spirits. The funeral procession to the grave was headed by the firecracker boys. Loud pops also scared off evil spirits. These boys were followed by boys carrying banners lauding the dead man. These in turn were followed by musicians fluting and drumming their grief. Finally came the huge coffin with its pallbearers. Secured on top of the coffin was a live rooster, a symbol of the man's spirit. Behind the coffin marched the men and boys of the family, all in the traditional mourning color of white. Any lack of enthusiasm for mourning on their part was more than made up for by the hired mourners who followed. These professionals bawled and wailed nonstop. Under their noses was some kind of gooey cotton to simulate a great gob of the tears and mucous that flowed. Behind them were men carrying paper images

81

of servants, houses, and livestock, all to be burned by the graveside and sent into the afterlife for the man's use. Then came the wives, who would some day be slid into the earth beside their husband as unceremoniously as possible. Last of all in the funeral procession trudged the man's worthless daughters.

"Oh, give me strength, Lord," prayed Gladys. "There is so much to do here in China."

As she walked through Yangcheng she saw Buddhist priests, heads shaved, wearing bright orange vestments. At the wedding the chanter had been a Taoist priest, robed in scarlet. Certainly Buddhism and Taoism seemed distinct religions. Just how did the Chinese balance these beliefs?

"I see signs of religion everywhere: Buddhist and Taoist, I guess," Gladys said to Jeannie, "but just what are the religious beliefs of these people?"

"Ahhh. . ." replied Jeannie. "You're on to a mighty slippery subject there. The truth is they have no core beliefs but their customs and Confucius."

"But the priests. . ."

"The Buddhist priests they ignore with as much indifference as they would ignore a college professor. The chanters at their weddings and funerals claim to be Taoists but they are really men trained in rituals and completely uneducated in Taoism."

"What then do the people believe?" asked Gladys.

"Their beliefs have two things common to Buddhism and Taoism. One is the belief that the supernatural consists of gods, ghosts, and ancestors. Second is the principle of 'ying-yang.' Everything in existence results from the combination of ying-yang. Yang is masculine: bright, warm, and dry. Ying is feminine: dark, cold, and wet. . ."

"I could have guessed," muttered Gladys.

Jeannie brushed off her comment. "Of course the Chinese all believe Confucianism, except that's no religion at all but a collection of proverbs for learning how to get along. And aside from what I've already mentioned, every region of China has its own special flock of gods and *'tu-di miao.'*"

"Tu-di miao?"

"Yes, little temples for their minor gods."

Gladys began to believe after a while that the common Chinese were not really very religious at all. Even though the poorest of the poor observed rituals, they seemed to honor them more from custom than religion. The real root of their Chinese-ness was, as Jeannie said, the rules or laws in Confucianism. Some were similar to Judaism:

> *Never do to others what you would not like them to do to you.*
>
> *Proper behavior to parents and elder brothers is the trunk of goodness.*
>
> *Show proper respect for the dead at the end and when they are far away.*
>
> *Respect the young.*
>
> *Learn to be faithful to your superiors and to keep promises.*

The rules of Confucianism were righteous, yet to Gladys they seemed only a pale form of Judaism, without the Jews' personal God. So what the Chinese believed fell short of Judaism and an eternity away from Christianity. The Chinese beliefs touted no love and no salvation, she was sure of that.

It made her even more determined to spread the gospel. She had been in Yangcheng for eight months and it was high time she mastered Chinese. She must study the language every spare moment, she told herself.

"Go for a walk with me," said Jeannie one afternoon after everything had quieted at the inn.

Gladys sighed as she sat at the table and studied long lists she had made of phonetically spelled Chinese words. "Thank you but I would really rather stay here and. . ."

"What!"

"I just meant I need the time to. . ."

"What!"

Jeannie's eyes were enlarged behind her spectacles, and appeared not innocent but almost murderously icy. Gladys had weathered her storms before, but this one seemed more ominous than any yet. Gladys smiled and rose.

"All right, I'll. . ."

"You needn't condescend!" screamed Jeannie. "I can see you're much too important to walk with an old washed up hag of a missionary, even if I have taught you everything you know, you ungrateful young snip."

"Oh, please, come now. . ."

"That's it then. Get out!"

Jeannie began throwing Gladys's belongings into the courtyard. Her white hair shot off her head like flames. Her eyes were wild. She never looked more like a devil to Gladys. Is that what the Chinese saw in her? Her illness had progressed dangerously far, Gladys knew that. Jeannie was behaving just as her mum's father had behaved many years ago in his furies, though his were not brought on by age but by alcohol.

As Jeannie continued to rage and throw things into the courtyard, Gladys slipped out and found Yang wide-eyed in the kitchen. He had heard the commotion.

"Mu yu fadze," he whispered with a shrug. "You must respect her. She is very old."

"But what will I do?"

"Go down to Tsechow for a while. I'll get a mule shanza for you."

"But. . ."

"Mrs. Jeannie will calm down and send for you. Be patient."

When Jeannie finally stormed out of the inn to take her walk, Gladys seized the opportunity to pack her things properly. Next she quietly waited away from the inn while Yang arranged the shanza for her. Then she left on a very glum journey. Was this the end of her work in Yangcheng? Certainly she had no resources herself. What would she do? Indeed, what could she do but return to Tsechow to stay with the elderly ladies at the mission?

Mrs. Smith was optimistic like Yang. "She'll take you back," she assured Gladys. "Wait and see. There will be a messenger from her in a day or two urging you to return."

Mrs. Smith's friend, the nurse, seemed to be biting her tongue. "Let us pray that is true," she volunteered weakly.

"You're holding back something," said Gladys bluntly.

"These things that affect the elderly are terribly hard to predict," said the nurse. "But Jeannie's case sounds very severe to me."

"Well, let's not upset Gladys," soothed Mrs. Smith. "I'm just sure there will be a message for her from Jeannie in day or two."

Mrs. Smith was partly right about the message coming. Three days later a message came from the yamen right in Tsechow. There was a rumor circulating that the white-haired foreign devil of Yangcheng was sick somewhere in the mountains.

"Not in Yangcheng?" worried Gladys.

"No," said Mrs. Smith. "It seems Jeannie is somewhere else."

The nurse sighed. "Poor Jeannie must have gone completely out of her head and just bolted off into the mountains." She looked at Gladys. "It was inevitable. It wasn't your fault. Now I'm sure this must be some kind of mental disorder."

Gladys left immediately, once again by mule. But this time she rode the mule, accompanied by a guide on another mule. There was no time to arrange a shanza. Besides the shanza was much slower than simply riding. They arrived in Chowtsun well before dark. Her guide questioned everyone who would talk to him. He came back to Gladys, looking very puzzled.

"They say the white-haired. . .woman is in Chin Shui."

"Chin Shui! Why, that's many miles northwest of Yangcheng—and mountainous miles at that."

How had Jeannie ended up at Chin Shui? Surely it was a manifestation of her illness. To abandon her beloved Inn of Eight Happinesses would have been unthinkable to her if she had been thinking straight. But Jeannie wasn't thinking straight. She was extremely ill mentally. Perhaps dead by now.

Gladys was very uneasy about proceeding into mountain country she did not know. The obstacles were many.

She would have to stay at inns where she wasn't wanted. Praise God, though, it wasn't winter. If she had to sleep out all night she could survive. The greatest danger was taking a fall on the steep trails. Bandits didn't concern her. She had heard of bandits but they were not common. They were summarily executed. Besides, God would protect her from any evil in her quest, she assured herself. She had to have faith.

Three days of riding through deep-gorged terrain finally took Gladys and her guide to Chin Shui. It was dusk when they reached the gate of the city. "Yes, yes!" screeched an excited resident. "There is a white-maned, phlegm-eyed foreign devil here all right. At an inn. Not inside but outside the walls. Very sick too. Be careful!"

The informant never really saw Gladys on the second mule. After all, she was just a woman. Soon they found the inn. The innkeeper was in the doorway, wringing his hands in despair. Several Chinese milled around him, commiserating. The innkeeper jumped when he realized Gladys was a second foreign devil and that she was going to enter his inn. Gladys rushed past him.

"Jeannie!" gasped Gladys in the courtyard of the inn.

Sprawled against a wall underneath the second-floor balcony was Jeannie. She appeared lifeless. Suddenly the old lady was illuminated by a paper-globed lantern Gladys's guide had requisitioned somewhere. Gladys was seized by horror. Decapitation was almost as easy to accept as the sight of Jeannie's disintegration. Her blue silk robe was bloody, as well as blackened by what must have coal dust from a nearby pile of coal. Still, there was no smell of death. Was she still alive?

"Jeannie, Jeannie," said Gladys softly near the old lady's ear.

"Yes," mumbled the old lady through lips cracked white with neglect.

"What happened?" asked Gladys foolishly.

Jeannie said nothing. It was doubtful she knew what happened. Gradually a story emerged, not from Jeannie, but from the disgruntled innkeeper. Jeannie had arrived by mule, not even with a guide, and imperiously commandeered a second-floor room. Then later while calling down from the balcony for food she had tumbled off the balcony. There was no railing on it as there was at the Inn of Eight Happinesses. She had landed on the pile of coal. She had been lying there several days. The innkeeper had given her some water but he was terrified of her. Now that he realized Gladys was going to care for the old lady, perhaps take her away, he became giddy with happiness.

"Get a litter," said Gladys to the guide. "We must get her to a room."

"No! No!" wailed the innkeeper. "Take the foreign devil away!"

But Gladys took possession of a choice lower-floor room. With the help of her guide she secured hot water and began to clean Jeannie. The old lady was badly bruised and cut up, with coal dust imbedded in her wounds. Her hands were shattered like crushed insects, probably because she broke her fall with them. Swelling and extreme tenderness to the touch revealed many other broken bones. And Gladys began to suspect a broken back, because Jeannie seemed virtually paralyzed. Still, the old lady clung to life. She even became coherent at times.

"Take me to Lu-an," she begged through pain. "There is a European doctor there."

And so Gladys did. But not before Jeannie had recuperated for six weeks in the inn. Gladys had never in her life seen a face happier than the innkeeper's when she left with Jeannie lying on a mule shanza. Her first guide had departed, so Gladys had to depend on a man from Chin Shui who was none too happy with the job.

Gladys was not pleased herself. Lu-an was sixty very hard miles to the northeast and took them even farther way from Yangcheng. And the same fears returned. Steep trails. Sheer cliffs. But after a very difficult week of traveling they found Lu-an. Gladys was told Lu-an was a prefectural city with officials ranking just below the staff of the great warlord Yen Hsi-shan's headquarters at Taiyuan. It was so strategic it had a hospital with English doctors and nursing sisters. At last Jeannie would have professional medical care.

"Frankly, she is very bad off," the doctor told Gladys. "She's a hardy woman to be sure or she wouldn't be alive now. But her days are numbered, I'm afraid. Her spinal injuries will keep her immobile and at her age she will waste away. I'm very sorry."

The doctor also mentioned the fact that Jeannie had a severe form of senile dementia. Her rages would only get worse. Still, she had lucid moments. It was during one of these rare moments that she summed it all up for Gladys.

"I don't want to die here, Gladys. Let's go back home to our Inn of Eight Happinesses."

So they returned by mule shanza to Yangcheng. All the way there Gladys listened to Jeannie rant and grow weaker.

Gladys fought the feeling of impending doom. How would she manage when Jeannie died? Surely she was not prepared to go it alone.

eight

The sight of Yangcheng filled Gladys with joy. "My joy is a wonderful surprise, Lord," she gasped. "What does it mean?"

Yang had kept the faith for many weeks. He still ran the inn, possibly because it allowed him to regale muleteers and their helpers with stories of Noah, of whom he was extremely fond. According to Yang now, Noah was the common thread who had done just about everything wonderful revealed in the Bible. Instead of self-righteous indignation, Gladys found only comfort in Yang's innocent enthusiasm.

Jeannie had called this place "home" and at the time Gladys had felt pity that the old lady would feel such a place was home. But now for the first time she realized she also felt this very exotic land was her home too. Yes, she loved Yangcheng and these innocent people. Jeannie would surely die, but Gladys would remain. But hadn't she known that all along?

"What could I have expected to happen, assisting a very old person?" she wondered.

The Chinese kept coffins in their houses. Coffins were possessions of pride for them. "See how well I've provided for myself," they seemed to say. Even this custom seemed quaint to Gladys now, not morbid as she once thought. And Jeannie's coffin of shiny black wood stood upright near her bed. It gave her comfort, although she was virtually mute now. She was almost Chinese now, this old lady, thought Gladys.

"But what am I thinking?" realized Gladys with a start. "It is the good news of the Gospel that must comfort Jeannie. The coffin is only a resting place, temporary at that, for her worn-out shell. Her soul will be with God." And she read from the Bible to Jeannie.

About noon on December 1, 1931, Jeannie died.

Her funeral was such an occasion that before the procession to the cemetery, the coffin, Jeannie inside, was placed in front of the inn in the bright sunshine. A banner proclaiming Jeannie's goodness ran the length of the black coffin. Flowers adorned it too. Yang arranged for a photographer. Gladys sat beside the coffin, stunned to see how many Chinese flocked to get into the photograph beside her, behind her, and before her. The image of Jeannie and her as foreign devils apparently was quite dead. Over thirty people, toddlers to bearded sages, wanted this honor. Their first guest at the inn, Hsi-Lien, was there too. He now hugged a copy of the Bible in Chinese that Hudson Taylor had provided many years before. Hsi-Lien had even learned to read tiny bits of it.

"And will you look at me?" gasped Gladys when she

saw the photograph later.

Sober-faced Gladys, in silk coat and trousers, hands clasped, was almost indistinguishable from the sober-faced Chinese ladies around her!

There was never a doubt in Gladys's mind after the funeral that with Yang she would continue to manage the inn. Her forced travel with a guide among the mountain people over several weeks had actually sharpened her understanding of the Chinese language. She was very comfortable now with her task.

All she had to do was polish more Bible stories. How the muleteers looked forward to them. Part of it of course was the childlike joy of staying up late, because most Chinese went to bed at dusk and awakened at dawn. But in the Inn of Eight Happinesses the guests gathered in the large room illuminated by several castor-oil lamps to listen to Bible stories.

"Perhaps you should visit the Mandarin and pay your respects," said Yang out-of-the-blue one day.

"The Mandarin?" answered a surprised Gladys.

Why had no one ever mentioned visiting this personification of local authority before? Certainly Jeannie had never considered visiting the Mandarin. What did this mean? Gladys wasn't sure. But she knew it was something to consider. Yang was not one to be frivolous. And she began to suspect some kind of face-saving going on here. Was the Mandarin curious about her? Had emissaries of the Mandarin put the idea into Yang's head? But why had it never happened before? Had the Mandarin been told old Jeannie with her wild fits of rage might be difficult? Had the Mandarin been told the young Gladys was mild-mannered?

A day later Yang mentioned it again. "Are you going to pay your respects to the Mandarin?"

"But I wouldn't know how to behave," she blurted.

Yang blinked. Yes, that was a problem. The next day he told Gladys no one seemed to know just how a foreign woman was supposed to behave. Every Chinese had a strict protocol with the Mandarin. But a foreigner? Yang seemed very agitated by this problem. Gladys was sure now people from the Mandarin were expecting him to persuade her to see the Mandarin. But all was at an impasse.

The next day the impasse was broken. "The Mandarin is coming! The Mandarin is coming!" screamed Yang. "You must get the front door!"

The exquisite timing was not lost on Gladys. All the mule teams had departed. None had yet arrived. Gladys became very self-conscious. Her fingers probed to see if her hair was neatly combed into a bun in back. Her robe was soiled, but she had none other that looked any better. Surely the Mandarin would recognize that she was an innkeeper. She watched the front door. Yang was nowhere in sight. That was significant. One did not presume to see the Mandarin unless the Mandarin approved such a meeting. So Yang was not part of this meeting, whatever its purpose.

"Welcome to the Inn of Eight Happinesses," said Gladys as she opened the front door with a great bow.

It was as if she had opened a flood gate. Through the front door paraded men in blue robes, some young, some graybeards. They were obviously attendants of some kind to the Mandarin. Finally in came a bright red and black sedan chair carried by nervous-looking servants. This entire affair with the foreign woman had everyone unsettled. It was without precedent.

The windows of the chair were curtained. The sedan chair was placed down in the exact center of the courtyard. One servant opened the door to the chair, almost bent double yet offering his arm to the passenger in the chair. The entire retinue was so sober, so stiff, that Gladys was unnerved.

"One dares not make a mistake in front of the Mandarin," gulped Gladys under her breath.

A tall man stepped out. He was as distinct from the others as a ruby among rough chunks of coal. He was a calm in the storm. His high-necked, wide-sleeved robe was brilliant red silk. His mustache dropped down at the corners. He wore a red skullcap, and a long braid went down his back.

He turned as if taking in the totality of the inn. When his gaze met Gladys's gawking eyes, who still stood open-mouthed at the front door, she realized she was being impertinent. She bent double so fast she almost tumbled over on her face. Now she could no longer see him, but she could hear him and his attendants approaching.

"Counsel on a certain subject would be helpful," someone said in very crisp yet refined *gwan-ha*, the official language.

"Oh, your Eminence?" she blurted nervously, not sure who was speaking to whom, yet grasping for formality. Did she dare look at the Mandarin?

"You may rise, foreign lady," said the crisp voice again. Apparently the appellation had not offended him.

Gladys stood straight, still lowering her eyes. She would take the greatest care. Yang's disappearance had set the tone. Besides, there was no humor, no warmth in this voice, only extreme refinement. She was sure now it was the Mandarin speaking. The brilliant red silk robe stood directly in front of her.

"For thousands of years," the voice said distinctly, "the feet of females have been bound since infancy."

"Yes, your Eminence," replied Gladys.

"The Kuomintang has decreed footbinding illegal," said the Mandarin, with just a tinge of irritation.

"Yes, your Eminence," repeated Gladys. Gladys knew the "Kuomintang" was the Nationalist Government headed by Chiang Kai-shek. But what had any of this to do with her?

"I am to stop the practice of footbinding as quickly as possible," emphasized the Mandarin. "My jurisdiction includes Chin Shui, Tsechow, Kaoping, Chowtsun, and Lingchuang, as well as Yangcheng. Someone representing me must go to all these places to inform the people of this new decree. But more is required. A woman must go to inspect and unbind all feet. To show it is not unknown for a woman to have such feet the woman should have unbound feet herself. Do you know of such a woman?"

"Such women are in China, Eminence."

"At my pleasure such a woman would receive a food allowance, a salary, a fine mule, and an escort of two armed guards. Do you know of such a woman?"

"I will write such women immediately advising them of your offer," said Gladys in desperation.

That very day Gladys wrote letters to everyone she knew in China. Surely someone could help the Mandarin. But deep inside she had her doubts. Any woman with unbound feet had to be European and it would be highly unlikely they would know this particular dialect well enough to carry out the Mandarin's wishes. The food allowance was millet. Most everyone preferred rice. She told Yang her concerns.

His eyes widened. "Miss Aylward, the Mandarin does not wish you to write every woman in China!"

"Well, for heavens sakes, just what am I to do?"

"Miss Aylward, he has called you to duty!"

"But I have responsibilities here."

"You cannot ignore the Mandarin's wishes. Are you going to ignore the Mandarin's wishes?" asked Yang, panic rising in his voice.

"Surely you are mistaken," commented Gladys.

But in her heart she realized Yang was right. Besides, she had worked in service. She knew an indirect order when she heard it. She was denying the truth of it because she didn't want to be a foot inspector. What would become of the inn?

But Yang wouldn't let it rest. If she didn't know who the Mandarin was before, Yang made sure she soon knew. Yang couldn't tell her how the Mandarin came to get his power, only that he had it. He was one of many district Mandarins to be sure, but still he answered only to the staff of Yen Hsi-shan, the warlord of all Shansi, in Taiyuan. And in his own district the Mandarin wielded the power of life and death over everyone. Yang told her that with particular emphasis. It came about as close to a direct statement that "if you don't do what the Mandarin says we will all die!" as he could make and still save face. He blinked as he waited for her response, as if thinking perhaps that saving face with this exasperating woman might not be possible.

"We will wait a little longer," said Gladys.

Yang remained at the inn but he seemed on the point of

97

flight all the time now. And he bolted when he heard the Mandarin was coming again. Gladys knew now that she had waited too long. But perhaps it was not too late to salvage her reputation with the Mandarin.

"Have you found a woman to inspect footbinding in my district?" the Mandarin asked bluntly.

"Your Eminence, I wanted to make sure you had the very best foot inspector possible, so I have written many letters. Not everyone has responded to my letters yet. . ."

"An excellent start," the Mandarin purred. "In the meantime I am sure you will want to assume the duty yourself." His tone allowed no objection. "I will instruct you how to do it. You will enter the village and read the decree from the Kuomintang. Next you will order all females to assemble. Then you will inspect all the women and girls. You will supervise the unbinding of the feet. Upon your return to Yangcheng you will submit a report to me at the yamen."

"Yes, your Eminence," said Gladys bowing deeply. She felt shamed. Then her heart filled with courage. She took a deep breath and said, "But while I am in these villages I will speak to the people about Jesus Christ." She couldn't risk looking at his face. Was he seething?

"You may speak of your philosophy if you wish," he said crisply. His tone of his voice implied her religion worried him not in the slightest. "The guards and the mules will arrive here tomorrow morning at dawn. I expect you will be starting your inspections right here in Yangcheng immediately."

"Gladly, your Eminence."

No one was happier with her decision than Yang. He

looked like a man given a reprieve from execution. Gladys was certain then that emissaries from the Mandarin had been asking him—probably daily—just when Yang would get this foreign woman to do what the Mandarin wished.

"I'll take good care of the inn," he promised. "And you know how I like to tell Bible stories."

When Gladys reflected on her new job she realized it was a gift from God. To think she had resisted. She had the opportunity to travel all over the Mandarin's district and meet every woman and girl of the many thousands in the district. It really was miraculous now that she accepted it. Why had she ever hesitated? Probably because she was single-minded and she could think of nothing but spreading the gospel to the male guests at the inn.

"But here is yet another way to spread the gospel," she realized. "And to women."

The next morning Gladys received the two guards and the mules in the courtyard. They bowed before her. Gladys bowed back. She began to load her small bag with a writing tablet and a few supplies but one of the guards quickly grabbed the bag and attached it to the saddle for her. It was obvious the Mandarin had instructed them to take good care of his ambassador to the district. The guards and mules seemed unnecessary when she was inspecting the environs of Yangcheng but perhaps their presence lent weight to her authority. Or perhaps the guards were to make sure she carried out her duties.

"Goodbye, Yang," she called as they left through the front gate.

"Goodbye, honorable Miss Aylward," he called, bursting with pride.

She was amazed to see Yang locked in a deep bow. Apparently she was someone to command respect now. They plodded off to begin the foot inspections.

She chose to start near the West Gate of Yangcheng and work east through the city. There were no actual inspections on the first day. The initial step had to be informing the neighborhood elders. Gladys made sure they understood the decree was from the Mandarin. When she returned at a specified time, no sooner than one day later, she expected every woman and girl to be waiting at a specified place.

The first time she returned to a neighborhood to the appointed place at the appointed time she understood the strength of the Mandarin's authority. A mob of fidgeting females awaited her, not that they looked very willing. They were obviously very frightened. How could this foreign woman be questioning a custom of thousands of years?

"Bring your baby to me," Gladys asked the first woman in line with an infant. Standing on a box so everyone could see her, Gladys unbound the tiny feet with great ceremony and massaged the baby's toes. "Now she will have strong healthy feet like mine!" said Gladys in a loud authoritarian voice.

To further make her point she took off her cloth shoes and let every woman and girl inspect her own feet if they wished. Their comments made it clear they had never seen a woman with such monstrously large feet. Gladys was amused. If she had worn size eight shoes instead of size three, would there have been a revolt? Surely many of the women would have fainted instead of just a few. The unbinding proceeded smoothly.

Her delay between reading the decree and returning to

inspect the feet was a stroke of genius. She knew the elders must have dashed to the yamen soon after she read the decree to them. "Is this foreign devil telling the truth?" they must have cried. "Yes. Don't make trouble for her," they were commanded. 'This decree is not only from the Mandarin but from Yen Hsi-shan, the warlord of all Shansi! And it is not only decreed by Yen Hsi-shan in Taiyuan but by the ruler of all China: Chiang Kai-shek, the Generalissimo himself!"

"How! How! How!" Gladys would shout after an unbinding, which meant "Good! Good! Good!"

And the toddlers, if not the infants could express their delight, after being unbound, the toes gently massaged by Gladys back to normal. Springing off the toes was pure joy to the tiny girls. Now they could jump! It was in the older girls that the depth of this cruel custom struck Gladys. For the feet of girls more than ten-years-old or so seemed beyond rehabilitation. All Gladys could do was to urge them to no longer bind their feet and to encourage them to try to uncramp the hideously deformed feet. Perhaps the bones of their feet still had enough youth in them to become almost normal feet someday. For the ultimate results of footbinding were tiny balled-up club feet!

"Praise You God for giving me this opportunity," prayed Gladys. "And forgive me for once thinking this task was an indignity below my station."

It was many weeks before Gladys actually went off to the outlying villages. The snows were gone. The air warmed. The Mandarin's expectation that she would begin in Yangcheng was not just a casual observation. Gladys realized that now. Yangcheng was the only practical starting point because of winter. There Gladys could work almost every day even if it snowed. But travel to the villages would have been very difficult, very inefficient, in winter.

Not only was the weather a good reason to wait to visit the more distant villages, but it was reasonable that by the time Gladys was ready to go the outer villages they would have heard of the decree. And they would have confirmed already that it was indeed from the Mandarin.

"Praise You, God," she prayed, "that You so gently persuaded me to proceed as the Mandarin seemingly so casually suggested."

Gladys was a very direct person, but she began to appreciate the subtleties of Chinese ways. What if she had stubbornly started with the villages first? It would have been folly. It would have exposed her as a silly simpleton in Chinese ways.

Statements from any Chinese had always to be weighed very carefully. Now just what did the speaker really mean? And no statement had to be weighed more carefully than one from the Mandarin or one of his emissaries. She was sure many a career in China had been destroyed or had been accelerated depending on a person's ability to detect subtle implications.

Another thing Gladys had thought much on. She must not become immune to their barbaric customs as Jeannie had. When Gladys first unbound tiny feet to discover the delicate toes curled grotesquely back under the feet, encroaching hideously into the sole of the baby's feet, she was sickened. She must never accept these cruel things, custom or not. She already knew of rumors of girl babies being murdered at birth. She must never get used to such outrages.

"Just as I must never forget I am here to spread the gospel of Jesus Christ," she reminded herself.

And to think that she, Gladys Aylward, was now bringing the Good News beyond Yangcheng to the outer villages. After nearly two thousand years the gospel had come to these remote mountains. And it was she, a tiny woman from a modest house on 67 Cheddington Road, delivering it in a sing-songy mountain dialect of Chinese. Was it possible that only two years before she had worked as a parlor maid in an English manor?

After a while it seemed to Gladys that no other world existed except this bright, elevated world of Shansi. And the world of Shansi accepted her. Now in Yangcheng people nodded at her shyly, instead of cursing her or glaring at her in silence.

People in the more remote villages were more reserved. Anyone or anything from the outside, other than mule trains, threatened their security. For they did not want help from the outside. Centuries of toil conditioned them to believe they had everything they wanted. An old proverb ran:

> *I plow my soil and eat.*
> *I dig my well and drink.*
> *For king or emperor*
> *what use have I?*

In fact, these villagers really did believe their beloved mountains provided everything. If one needed coal, it was there. One dug at a seam of coal in the mountainside and filled a bucket. If one needed land for crops, with hard work a field could be terraced out of the mountainside.

What little they lacked came in regularly by mule trains. Weren't the mules and muleteers also of the mountains? The mountains seemed inexhaustible. Gladys came to appreciate the independence of these outer villages.

"What if one could truly shut off the outside world?" she mused. "Might one be better off without wars and disease?"

After all, Gladys was completely independent of any mission society herself—just as Jeannie Lawson had become toward the end. Gladys's mission society was Yang and the Inn of Eight Happinesses.

But occasionally the outside world intruded. Mrs. Smith had taken it upon herself to send Gladys a convert, Lu-Yung-Cheng. He was even paid by Mrs. Smith. To refuse his help would have been cold ingratitude. And Gladys found she didn't mind his help at all. Lu-Yung-Cheng's knowledge of Christianity was far more pure than Yang's. So now Gladys didn't worry so much that when she off in some distant village Yang was telling stories with impunity about Noah driving the moneychangers out of the Temple.

Once when she was back in Yangcheng, a messenger stormed into the inn. "Come right away," he wailed. "There's a riot at the jail!"

"What does that have to do with me?" asked Gladys.

"Come right away. It's an official order." He flapped a piece of paper wildly.

Gladys saw that he did indeed carry a sheet of red paper. She knew by now that meant some kind of message from the yamen. The messenger was apoplectic. What was he going to do with this foreign devil if she refused? Surely the authorities would blame him. This was an emergency.

His head might roll if he failed. He was so upset he bypassed all the normal subtleties of Chinese communication. Gladys realized his dilemma, shrugged, and indicated she would proceed to the jail.

She was certainly not prepared for the what she heard as she approached the jail. Screams of rebellion! Or were they screams of chaos?

The warden of the jail was at the door of the jail waiting. "You must go in and stop the fighting among the prisoners," he blurted to Gladys.

"Are there any guards trapped inside with the prisoners?"

"No."

"Then why not let it run its course?" she asked calmly.

"The prisoners are killing each other," the warden cried.

"Killing each other?" Gladys tried to remain calm. Surely this was an exaggeration. "Then send your soldiers inside and restore order."

"We do not have enough soldiers. The prisoners have completely taken over the courtyard inside."

"But why me?" gasped Gladys in exasperation.

"They tell me you preach everywhere that your God is a Living God who protects you," said the warden.

"But. . ."

"Well, is your God all powerful or not? Do you really believe what you preach or not?" he plied.

"But this is so unfair. . ." she muttered, her voice trailing off.

nine

The warden slumped. "Then your God is not all powerful. You don't really believe what you preach."

"No, I do believe," murmured Gladys.

Of course there was a crowd around the jail now because of the commotion. Gladys and her Christianity were on trial. Had the warden truly wanted her help out of desperation? Or had some slyer mind figured out that this misfortune could be used in a way to expose the foreign devil's Christianity as a fraud? She was very angry inside for being maneuvered into such a hopeless situation. *Oh please God,* she prayed, *make me calm enough to think! Lord, give me courage and wisdom.*

The crisis and its significance to her mission crystallized. Did Christ's apostles wish to be put into impossible situations? Did all the Christian martyrs through the centuries wish to be put into impossible situations? No, crises came to them without warning. And a crisis had come to her without warning.

"I will go into the jail," she announced loudly. "But only through the help of Jesus Christ will I prevail! For the gospel of God in our Bible says, "I can do all things through Christ which strengtheneth me."

Faith. Faith. Faith. She chanted this word with each step she took to walk inside the walls of the jail and then through a passageway to the courtyard. She must believe. At the end of the day would her Lord shout of her "Verily, I say unto you, I have not found so great faith," as he did about the Roman centurion? Wasn't she in the day of the Lord?

By the time she reached a massive gate in the passageway that ran into the courtyard she was calm. Hysterical screams came from inside the courtyard. The one jail guard at the massive gate looked rattled.

Gladys said, "Open the gate. Let me go in."

The guard opened the gate. She took a deep breath and forced herself to walk through the gate, which clanged shut behind her. She walked the rest of the way to the opening into the courtyard. There she stopped, numbed at the sight. The prisoners had not seen her. She seemed to be floating, free for the time being to take in the sight of the battle.

The courtyard square was about sixty feet on a side, each side a wall of barred cells. The prisoners, perhaps fifty in all, were in state of total hostility to each other, every one poised to spring any direction, intensely alert to each other's movements. Each seemed to occupy a tiny territory about ten feet square. Whatever had already transpired had resulted in several prisoners lying in the dirt. Some might have been beaten unconscious. One had a gaping crimson wound in his skull. Blood pooled under his head. Was he already dead?

"Ah, there is the center of the fracas," Gladys told herself.

One man clutched a meat cleaver, ready to strike. The cleaver had blood on it. No one else had a weapon, as far as Gladys could tell. The man with the cleaver feinted at his neighbor with his deadly weapon. His intended victim darted away, warily watching all his neighbors too. The man with the cleaver was not acting defensively. He was eyeing potential victims. Still, there was no unity against the man and his deadly weapon. They all seemed degraded beyond a pack of wild animals.

Suddenly the atmosphere seemed to change. There was something new in their predicament: Gladys.

"Lao-yang-kwei," she heard someone say.

One pair of eyes after another noticed the "foreign devil" standing at the opening. Only the man with the cleaver seemed not to notice her. He was too busy looking for his next victim. One assault brought him close to Gladys. Suddenly he was not ten feet away, glowering at her. Her freedom had ended—now she had to act. *God, do Your will,* she prayed.

She stepped into the courtyard. "Hand that cleaver to me!" she commanded.

His face seemed to almost explode as he hesitated. Should he strike this foreign devil? Suddenly his face dissolved into meekness. He handed her the cleaver.

"Now, all of you stop shouting," she barked. "Form ranks in front of me!"

They formed ranks. Half a dozen remained on the ground. Several crept out of cells they had been hiding in. The stark danger over, Gladys now digested the sight of the prisoners themselves.

They were the most pitiful people she had ever seen. They had sunk far below poverty. Their clothing seemed nothing but tattered rags. And if the fabric had color once, it now was gone. Except for fresh blood stains, the material was the color of dirt.

The prisoners were cadaverously thin. Their shaved heads exposed scabs, and their faces were blotched with blood, disease, and hopelessness. Gladys knew they crawled with lice, and they smelled of vomit and worse. The salty smell of blood was on them too.

It was all Gladys could do to summon the strength to scold this human rubbish. But she must keep them under control. One moment of weakness and one man might ignite the others. They were pitiful but not without sin.

"Do you have no shame?" she growled. "Look at you. A flock of chickens has more dignity."

"We have no purpose. . ." mumbled a man in the front row.

"Oh, stop feeling sorry for yourself! Let's see if we can't straighten out this mess you've made. Clean up the courtyard and the warden will be in a better mood when he metes out justice. Perhaps he will be lenient. After all, you've only hurt yourselves with your foolishness."

Gladys paused. Somehow something positive must be gained from this tragedy—not for herself but for the prisoners. Perhaps the warden was interested only in gaining control of the prisoners again, but she had other interests. She remembered now the words of Christ Himself: *I was . . .sick, and in prison, and ye visited me not.* This was surely a directive to her as well as all Christians.

Something very important was happening at the jail for Gladys this day. She reminded herself how her mind had resisted the messenger's call for help. What a hypocrite she would have been if she had refused to help!

She assumed a positive air. Great things were going to happen from this tragedy. "Appoint a spokesman," she demanded of the prisoners. "I wish to talk with him while the rest of you clean up this mess."

The spokesman they selected was Feng. Gladys learned Feng was once a Buddhist priest, now a convicted thief. He was serving an eight-year sentence. Feng knew only that the fight started over the cleaver itself. The prisoners were allowed to use it for an hour or so to cut up food. Perhaps someone used it too long. Perhaps someone took it out of turn. Who could know now? The dead men would certainly not tell their stories.

Food was always a volatile matter on every prisoner's mind. The jail itself supplied no food. Food was supplied only by relatives or friends. Some men almost starved. Food was all they thought about.

"What do you do during the day?" asked Gladys.

"Nothing," answered Feng hollowly. "We wait for time to pass. Occasionally one of us is removed to be executed. Occasionally one of us serves out his sentence and leaves. More often, one of us dies from disease and then a gang of us chained together take him down the mountainside at night to bury him."

Suddenly the courtyard was full of guards and jail officials, including the warden. He was too shrewd a man to be heavy-handed now. He assumed a look of uncompromising sternness though, as he watched the prisoners tidy up

110

the courtyard. But Gladys could see he was very relieved to be in command again.

Gladys drew him aside. "I am sure the Mandarin would be pleased to learn the fighting not only stopped but it inspired you to improve the conditions of the jail."

"Improve the jail?"

"You must give these men work."

"You are foreign. You do not understand. We have very strict guilds in Shansi that prevent unauthorized work. The Mandarin himself presides over the allotments!"

"There must be some work they can do. Don't you see that if they could earn a little money they could buy food for themselves. Maybe even clothing. Straw for their cells. They would be a far happier group. If you suggest this to the Mandarin then maybe he can decide what kind of work might be available."

"This is very unusual," mulled the warden.

"Perhaps I could make the suggestion to the Mandarin," said Gladys carelessly.

"No!" blurted the warden.

"Perhaps you will do it then?"

"Yes."

"One more thing. . ." Gladys saw the warden cringe as if he expected her to gloat over her triumph in the courtyard. Her God was indeed all powerful. But Gladys had become too subtle for such gloating. "I promised the prisoners you would be lenient. I wish no one to be punished for this incident."

His face fell. "But some men are dead."

"If you wish me to lose face with the prisoners, then go ahead and punish some of them. But when you have your next problem here don't send for me. They would have no faith in me a second time."

He blinked. "I suppose a few dead men wouldn't cause too much consternation with the Mandarin if they were killed while fighting each other." He looked at her expectantly.

"Such a thing is probable."

"Then it's settled."

Gladys waited patiently for the warden to handle the affair with the Mandarin. Meanwhile Gladys began to visit the jail. She brought them the Good News of Jesus Christ. She encouraged hygiene. She had to bolster the prisoners until some kind of reform could begin.

Although the warden would have preferred all the credit himself for handling the outbreak and Gladys seemed to want no credit for herself, the rumor spread that it was the tiny foreign lady who had smothered the rebellion. The warden had challenged her Living God right out in the open. There had been many witnesses. And somehow the tiny lady had entered the jail and stopped a pack of murdering thugs. Only a fool would not know this tiny woman was an *"Ai-Weh-Deh,"* a "Virtuous One."

"Chi-la fan ma, Ai-Weh-Deh?" seemed to echo from every doorway now when Gladys passed.

"Chi-la," she responded over and over.

One day the warden intercepted her at the jail. He bowed. "The Mandarin was pleased with my plan, Ai-Weh-Deh. He suggested that if somehow I could obtain an old loom, it would be all right for the prisoners to make enough cloth for their own shoes and puttees. If they made a few extra puttees they could sell them. No one likes to make puttees. And perhaps the prisoners could find some way to grind corn. There's a need for that in Yangcheng."

It wasn't long before the prisoners had two old looms making coarse cotton fabric, some of which they used to make their own shoes. The rest they used to make puttees, the ankle wrap that secured the bottoms of trousers. The puttees they sold. The grinding of corn started with simple grinding stones, then evolved into a mill wheel powered by plodding prisoners.

Much of the equipment was wheedled from merchants by Gladys. The well-to-do Chinese did not refuse this Ai-Weh-Deh out of hand now. The prisoners were delighted when she lugged in two rabbits, a buck and a doe. After all, the rabbits were needed to tidy up all the grain they spilled while milling. And who could not guess how the rabbits would multiply themselves?

Feng's eyes soon glowed with hope. "The extra rabbits certainly yield tasty meat and warm furs."

Perhaps nothing she accomplished was appreciated more by the prisoners than the time she got them out of their four walls. Occasionally now she was able to persuade the warden to chain the prisoners together so they could be marched out into blessed space—with no dead to bury and with the sun on their faces. They wanted nothing more than to clank down the street out of one of the city gates and stand at the deeply rutted trail's edge. There they gazed off at the plunging valleys and green mountain tops. No walls. No bars. No chains. Yes, this great space was what they lived for.

"Someday we will all be free again," vowed Feng for the entire group.

The more Gladys was accepted into the officialdom of Yangcheng, the more compassionate to the poor she became, because she saw how well the upper level Chinese officials lived, even in Yangcheng. They and no one else enjoyed lavish twenty-course meals. Each course consisted of four choices. Bird's nest soup, shark fin soup, candied sweets, sugared lotus seeds, dozens of delicacies pickled, limed eggs, sea slugs, chicken, beef, pork, on and on. Meanwhile, many of the poorest of the poor ate only millet and wild dates in the hardest times.

"If they are lucky they might have green fruit that someone else discarded," reflected Gladys who had eaten some hard pears and peaches herself. "If they are unlucky they eat nothing and die."

The officialdom—and no one else—enjoyed plays given by itinerant acting troupes. In a small, well-lit theater they smoked cigarettes or water pipes as they watched the play unfold. Stage props were rare; all but a few objects were conveyed by pantomime. All characters—male or female—were played by men, faces black or red if evil, white if good, who cried out their lines in falsetto. If a "good" actor was killed in the plot he reposed on a table that represented heaven. if an evil actor was killed he fell to the floor, and slithered off to the depths.

The play was invariably accompanied by music, usually delivered by a drum and a two-stringed fiddle. Gladys had long noticed Chinese music had a five-note scale, but what it lacked in range it gained in melody. Most songs rarely repeated motifs like Western music but varied throughout. Outside the rigid format of the plays, musical instruments were much more diverse: flutes, mouth organs, chimes, stringed zithers, drums, bells, and many varieties of two-stringed fiddles.

To Gladys, Chinese music seemed embodied in the simple scales of fiddles and flutes. Although the poorest of the poor heard music of some kind, certainly they knew nothing of plays, night-time or otherwise. At night they crawled onto their kang—heated or not—when the sun went down.

"'For ye have the poor always with you. . .' are the Lord's own words in Matthew," reflected Gladys.

How often in England she had heard that portion of Bible verse quoted out of context to dismiss the problem of the poor. And it was certainly an attitude that she found among the well-to-do in China. But Gladys knew the Lord had not meant that at all. In fact He had alluded to God's words in Deuteronomy 15:11: "For the poor shall never cease out of the land," in which God went on to say, "therefore I command thee, saying, Thou shalt open thine hand wide unto thy brother, to thy poor, and to thy needy."

Fighting pride, always trying to give all credit to God, Gladys had to marvel how her ministry was growing. It was only 1933. Jeannie had been dead little more than one year. Gladys ministered to the passing mule trains. Because of her job as foot inspector, she ministered in Yangcheng and beyond in the other villages. And now she ministered in the jail in Yangcheng. Naturally this must be extended into jails all over her district.

But she had more than pride to fight. Complacency was a trick of her spiritual enemy too. She had to fight off the feeling that there were no more wrongs she could address. Still, she did not have to seek the wrongs. They seemed to come to her. "Because not I, but God, is the master of history," she had to admit.

115

One day she was going to the yamen in Yangcheng to report to the Mandarin on her trip as foot inspector to one of the outer villages. She had been brooding over the plight of women. Everywhere they were treated as little more than livestock. The brides came into the husband's household as property. They were beaten. Girl babies were quietly murdered. She was sure of that now because there were just too few among the people of Shansi. As foot inspector, shouldn't she bring the Mandarin's attention to such terrible treatment of women? The Mandarin was a man of great refinement. And he was buffered at all times. Perhaps he really did not realize how horribly women were treated. Wasn't this a new China he administered? But would he consider an unforgivable affront? She had already accomplished so much. . . .

She stopped abruptly. "Is that your child?" she demanded of a woman sitting against a wall.

The woman's face was shiny from neglect. Her hair was plastered down. Although her earrings were silver and her ankles were secured by bright green puttees, she otherwise looked poor. Her dirty clothing was the common high-necked tunic over baggy pants. But the woman was immaculate compared to the child slumped against her. The child wore only a filthy loincloth. Sores covered the face and head. The belly was swollen from eating nothing. How old was the child? Three? Four? *Forgive me, God,* Gladys prayed, her thoughts almost a scream of pain, *but I can't even tell if it is a boy or a girl!*

"Is that your child?" she asked again.

"Are you talking to me?" the woman crabbed.

"Yes, that child looks very sick."

"Well, what is that to you?"

Neither Gladys nor this woman knew anything of saving face. Their contact was pure hostility. Who was this woman? Gladys asked herself. Was she from the mountains? She showed no affection for the child. Was she one of the notorious child sellers? If so, then the child must have been a girl. Boys were far too precious for a woman such as this bedraggled wretch to be dragging around.

"Do you want to buy this child or not?" asked the woman.

"I see!" snapped Gladys.

"The price is cheap. Two silver dollars."

Gladys was ready to explode. She moved on to the yamen. This was definitely something she could tell the Mandarin about. The plight of women in general would have to wait. She bowed as she entered his presence.

"Chi-la fan ma, Ai-Weh-Deh?" he asked pleasantly.

"Chi-la. Thank you, Eminence," she responded. *"Chi-la fan ma?"*

"Oh, *chi-la,* thank you. And your old ones, Ai-Weh-Deh, are they well?"

"Very well, Eminence. And yours?"

"Very well, Ai-Weh-Deh."

The many pleasantries this time only aggravated her as she waited for a chance to speak things of substance. Still, one didn't neglect propriety with a man like the Mandarin. Gladys reported on her trip to one of the outer villages. The condition of the women's feet in the village was very compliant with the new decree, she assured him. This was the juncture where she had agonized over whether or not to launch her protest against the treatment of women. But God had given her no choice today.

"There is a woman very near here trying to sell a child," she said bluntly.

"Don't interfere, Ai-Weh-Deh. Selling children is wicked, but if you interfere with the woman she is likely to do something terrible to the child. So when you leave here you are go to the opposite side of the street and *see nothing. . .*"

"But. . ."

"And you will *say nothing* of this conversation to anyone. You may leave, Ai-Weh-Deh."

"I came to China to answer the call from Jesus Christ," she said hotly. "I will not respect customs that are an affront to His love!"

She exited rapidly. She felt hot but sick. How would the Mandarin take this disrespect? At least no one else had been present. Perhaps he would forgive her. She would pray for God's help in the matter. She must take her chances. Besides it was as if the wrath of God had spoken through her. She certainly would *not* go to the other side of the street to avoid the evil woman. In fact she would see just how far she could push the woman.

Gladys had only ninepence in coppers in her pocket. If it was God's will she would somehow save the child with that paltry sum. "How much do you want for the child?" she snapped at the woman.

"I told you before. Two dollars."

"I don't have two dollars."

"One dollar then," snapped the woman bitterly.

Gladys refused. After much angry haggling—for neither of these two women desired to save face for the other— Gladys walked back to the Inn of Eight Happinesses penniless but carrying a very sick child. Perhaps the woman had realized the child was so close to dying she might not ever get any money for the poor thing.

Yang was astonished. "This child is almost dead." His tone carried a reprimand.

"Get a bowl of millet."

"That child could bring us trouble," he grumbled as he went to the kitchen.

Yang returned to place the bowl down near the child. The skinny limbs of the toddler sprang to life to snatch the bowl, then to run off into a corner. There sloppy handfuls of millet were gobbled down in a flash. Then the child licked the bowl and its own hands until not one grain remained.

Gladys nicknamed the child "Ninepence." But her pleasure was blunted by the child's hostility. Day after day the child was little more than a wild animal. Any attempt to wash it or dress it was met with scratching and biting and kicking and screaming. The food made it stronger and wilder yet. After three weeks of praying for God's help, Gladys had an idea. She knew of a woman who had lost her baby. The woman was mired in grief.

"I have a child at the Inn of Eight Happinesses," she told the woman. "I need the help of a real mother."

What invisible forces passed between the grieving mother and the savage child? What sweet cooing from the mother penetrated the child's defenses? What look in the mother's eyes melted the child's heart? Gladys could not fathom how it happened. But she was sure it was the love of Christ that transformed the girl. Because somehow in a few hours the mother transformed the filthy, savage child into a fresh-scrubbed, well-dressed, docile girl.

119

They learned the child was not three or four years of age but a very undersized six. The little girl even smiled. Gladys had hoped the mother would take the child. But no. She could not do it. Her husband would never allow it. He might even do something bad to the girl.

"So, God has decided she stays here," said Gladys to Yang. "Ninepence is all right as a nickname, but I'm going to christen her Mei-en."

"'Beautiful Grace' is a good name," agreed Yang. No one was more amazed, or pleased, with the miraculous transformation of Mei-en than the Doubting Thomas: Yang.

Ninepence showed every sign of remaining sweet and demure. She was everything Gladys wanted in a daughter. But the firestorm over Ninepence had involved the Mandarin too. Gladys had been very abrupt with him, very rude.

The next time she went to the yamen to report to him about a foot inspection she was extremely worried. She was not relieved simply because he received her without any apparent change in their routine of civilities. He was far too disciplined to show his disapproval before the usual courtesies.

But after her report, he did broach the subject, unsmiling.

ten

"They tell me you purchased the child on the street," said the Mandarin, his face unreadable.

"Mei-en is my daughter now, Eminence," replied Gladys.

"They tell me she was as wild as a wolf." Was the Mandarin almost smiling?

"It was the ferocity of God bringing her back to life."

"Perhaps." He paused.

She excused herself. She had learned to do that when he first paused. It was her signal to leave. But the Mandarin had made no complaint about her disobedience. In fact in his own cool way he seemed friendlier than ever before. Ninepence was definitely a gift from God.

One day Ninepence came to her at dinner time. "Are we having a nice meal?"

Gladys could scarcely keep from laughing. "Of course we are having a nice meal."

"If I ate less of the meal, could you also eat less of it?"

"Less, less, less. What are you up to?"

"There is a boy at the gate who has nothing to eat. We can give him our two 'lesses.'"

"Well, bring him to dinner."

The boy was about eight, dressed in ragged clothes, not nearly warm enough for the winter. He was from a tiny village far east of Yangcheng. Bandits had raided the hamlet and killed his father. His pregnant mother took him and tried to trek to relatives who lived in the mountains. But she went into labor on the trail and died. A mule train brought the boy into Yangcheng where he begged on the streets.

He was open-faced, with not a hint of guile. Nor did he show a trace of self-pity. Gladys didn't doubt his story for a moment. It was so sad it tore at her heart.

"You will stay with us from now on," she told the boy. Inspired by Ninepence's introduction she nicknamed the boy "Less."

Gladys began to suspect Ninepence's chief occupation in life was now to seek out abandoned urchins. One day the following spring Ninepence and Less appeared with a toddler in tow. This child was about two years old, with that blinking, bewildered look that all abandoned innocents wear. He seemed too small to just suddenly appear, though. Gladys thought he might be lost.

At her request the Mandarin had the Town Crier broadcast the boy's dilemma. No one claimed him. He became the third child Gladys took in. Or was he in reality the second child Ninepence took in? At any rate the name Gladys gave him revealed her true feeling for this new child.

"You are 'Bao Bao,' " she said, "My 'Precious Bundle.' "

One day when Gladys gave her report to the Mandarin he never paused to indicate to her the audience was over. This time he kept the conversation going. Was the shrewd man leading up to some new dangerous duty for her? His topics included polite inquiries about Gladys and England, Gladys and the jail, and Gladys and her adopted children.

Then he mused, "Ai-Weh-Deh, you come here on a mission to people you consider barbarians, don't you?"

"Not barbarians, Eminence."

"Yet our civilization is older by far than yours," he continued. "Scholars say Britain was a land of grunting, fur-clad savages when the ancient Chinese sat in silk robes, listening to orchestras of chimes and zithers, and composing poetry."

"Perhaps that isn't the way we Christians look at it, Eminence," she replied politely. "The Jews, the people we consider the Chosen People, the people from whom sprang our Savior, were also at this ancient time listening to stringed instruments and composing their own poetry while sitting in many-colored robes." She paused to smile. "Although I admit at this ancient time we British were probably running about in animal skins."

"The lines of our most ancient poetry, 'Shijing,' are arranged in stanzas. Each line has four syllables and rhymes with another line." He smiled slyly. "Tell me about this Jewish poetry."

Gladys explained how Jewish poetry was usually in couplets expressing the same thought in two different ways. There was no express meter or rhyme. The greatest collection of Jewish poetry was the Book of Psalms, which Christians read and sang regularly.

The Mandarin said, "So in that way you do honor to

the most ancient of your traditions? Most enlightening."
He paused, very pleased with this insight. "Perhaps we
Chinese are also wrong in considering you Westerners
complete barbarians. . ."

The Mandarin had become philosophical. Gladys was
shocked. Had she moved up to a new level in his estima-
tion? Was not this kind of soft, polite bantering that now
followed their official business reserved for friends of
some stature? This polite but probing kind of conversation
seemed to please him more than anything. But why should
she be surprised? He apparently considered himself a
scholar as much as a governor.

Perhaps in that respect the Chinese had carried more of
their tradition forward than the British did. Britain had not
had such men for a very long time. The great universities
of Oxford and Cambridge still tried to provide a classic
education for those who wanted it, but Gladys suspected
the men who wanted it never went on to also govern.

"Perhaps Ai-Weh-Deh would like to hear my own un-
interesting history," he mused.

"Of course, your Eminence!" she blurted.

The Mandarin went on to tell her about himself. He
came from the northern plateaus of Shansi. His well-to-do
father sent him to school at the age of six. There from a
primer called the *Three Character Classic* he copied five
hundred characters of the Chinese language on to rice paper
with a sable brush until he had memorized each one. The
text told of a son's duties and the need for an education.
This book had been the Chinese introduction to literacy for
one thousand years!

Most Chinese boys stopped after mastering the *Three*

Character Classic. "But I was fortunate," said the Mandarin. "My father had enough money to allow me to go further. So next I had to master another five books like the first one."

Then he told Gladys how he then conquered the four great books of Confucius: the "Shih Shu." These sayings of Confucius and his followers contain the foundation of Chinese morality and politics. Anything contrary to these sayings was deemed false. In conjunction with the four books he and other students had to develop skills at prose and poetry, displayed in elegant free-hand calligraphy. Attaining this level was an accomplishment recognized by the rank "Cultural Talent."

Then he moved on to the ultimate mastery of Confucianism: the "Wu Ching" or "Five Classics." Some of these originated from Confucius but some were more ancient. Included were "I Ching" a manual of divination, and "Li Chi," the source for all principles of public and private conduct. Finally he was deemed a "Finished Scholar."

This in no way made him a Mandarin. A Mandarin was a district magistrate, empowered by a warlord. But possessing the scholarly credentials of a Finished Scholar made him well qualified to be a magistrate.

"I underestimated Confucianism," admitted Gladys to the Mandarin.

But she still considered it a pale form of Judaism, a mere wisp of Christianity. Where was the love that was in Judaism? Where was the redemption that was in Christ? Where was the promise of eternity offered by the Trinity? Still, she appreciated the Mandarin opening up to her. Was he troubled about something? How could she broach such a possibility?

"Do you see good times ahead for Shansi, your Eminence?"

"Aaah, Ai-Weh-Deh, you are most perceptive." He almost frowned. "I have heard many things in recent months. Things most people of Shansi know nothing about. Things they would not care to hear anyway because they think they live in the protected heart of China."

"I heard a rumor the great Yellow River flooded. Thousands drowned and starved. Is that what you mean?"

"You are ignorant too? Do you not know Japan has invaded Manchuria? Oh, it has been glossed over by the Kuomintang because it is very embarrassing to be stepped on. But the Japanese are there and they won't be satisfied with just Manchuria. Then there are our own Chinese Communists—as rabid a pack of wolves who ever roamed the Chinese wilderness—biding their time far to the south in the Jinggang Mountains of the Jianxhi province. The Communists believe in nothing elevated—not Confucianism, not Buddhism, not Taoism, not your Christianity. They worship themselves. They promise the peasants land and booty. . ."

"You make it all sound very menacing."

"I am very troubled because the Kuomintang made wonderful promises too but never kept them."

Gladys could convey no comfort to the Mandarin. Her concerns were too mundane for such a worrier. Besides, as much as she appreciated his friendship, his refinement, his just ways, he represented an old, corrupt, very privileged way to her. He ate the finest foods. He indulged himself in the best entertainment available. And worst of all his ways, he was profligate. Besides his "number-one" wife he had other wives, not unusual for men with wealth—although Gladys in no way approved. But worse yet, he also had concubines, a very sinful indulgence enjoyed only by the wealthiest of men. Worst of all, he had for his pleasure women who weren't even considered concubines but outright slaves! It made her want to disobey him.

And yet, did not Paul advise Christians to obey authorities? He wrote it in his letter to the Romans:

> *Let every soul be subject unto the higher powers. For there is no power but of God: the powers that be are ordained of God. Whosoever therefore resisteth the power, resisteth the ordinance of God. . . for this cause pay ye tribute also: for they are God's ministers, attending continually upon this very thing. Render therefore to all their dues: tribute to whom tribute is due; custom to whom custom; fear to whom fear; honour to whom honour. . .*

Oh, how terribly difficult the Holy Scripture was to understand sometimes. She read the passage a second time. There it was: God's words to obey the authorities. But in her own case, suppose she opposed the Mandarin's authority? Would life be worse for her charges or better? The answer was clear.

One day Less came to Gladys. "A man was hanging around the children when school was let out. He tried to talk to Ninepence but I grabbed her and we ran away."

"Oh no!"

Less was very protective of Ninepence. But he was no

match for a grown man. So Gladys went to the Mandarin. He agreed to post a soldier near the school when it let out for the day. The threatening man was a dolt because the very next day he again grabbed Ninepence after school. Less tore into him like a tiger but it was the soldier's rifle that subdued him. The man said he had been hired by the girl's uncle to bring her back to the mountain village where she had been born. It seemed she was somehow in line to inherit something.

"Grabbing her off the street is a peculiar way to inform her of a possible inheritance," reflected the Mandarin privately to Gladys. "It seems more likely the man was paid to remove her from any possible inheritance. No doubt when the uncle sold her he never expected to hear of her again. The muleteers must have talked to the uncle about the little girl who lived with Ai-Weh-Deh, the same little girl who had been sold to Ai-Weh-Deh by a nasty woman from their village."

"Does the uncle have a claim on her, Eminence?"

"That is but one item to be settled. The other item to be settled is whether or not she has some kind of inheritance the uncle doesn't want her to get. We will have a trial to settle everything once and for all. I will be the magistrate."

Gladys did little more than bring Ninepence to court at the yamen. There they responded to the Mandarin's questions, each question postscripted by a broad hint of how he wanted the question answered. At the trial's end Gladys was officially Ninepence's guardian. And Ninepence had an inheritance of many silver dollars. It was a fortune to most Chinese. It was small wonder that the uncle had panicked and tried to have Ninepence abducted and killed.

Gladys promised to put the money aside for her education or dowry, whichever she wished.

But Ninepence was not particularly happy about it. Such a past she had discovered for herself! And with it came grief. Apparently her mother and father were dead. Even her grandparents. But pain had seared all her memories of them away. She could remember nothing. But now she grieved.

"Praise You, God, for sending me Your wisdom through Paul's words," was all Gladys could think of. "I shudder to think what would have happened to my precious Ninepence if I had spurned the Mandarin out of self-righteousness. . ."

In 1934 the Mandarin informed Gladys that the Nationalists under Chiang Kai-shek were ruthlessly hounding the small remnant of Communists in south China. The Communists were certainly evil by all accounts, but try as she might, Gladys could not appreciate their threat to Shansi. After all, the Communists were a thousand miles away, more or less, in the Jinggang Mountains of the Jianxhi province.

"But you seem unhappy, Eminence," she observed.

"The Communists are fleeing in this direction. There are political elements not that far northwest of us that might welcome them."

And Gladys learned many months later that the few thousand Communist survivors had been welcomed at Yenan to the northwest—no more than two hundred miles from Yangcheng! After that fact was revealed to her she never again dismissed anything as insignificant that the Mandarin told her. Even her statement to the Mandarin that the

Communists were separated from Yangcheng by the raging Yellow River came back to haunt her one winter. Yangcheng was in the midst of a winter that even "four-layers" would not handle. Everyone was so bloated by padded layers of clothing they looked like great blue billiard balls bouncing off one other. The charm of that wintry spectacle soon soured.

"The Communists are fighting our Nationalists at Taiyuan," announced the Mandarin during one of Gladys's visits.

"Communists? Here in northern Shansi! But how can that be?"

"This winter is so cold the Yellow River froze over, Ai-Weh-Deh. The Communists simply walked across on the ice!"

The situation worsened. Some Communist soldiers actually entered Yangcheng. The Mandarin instructed his handful of soldiers not to engage them. Gladys realized then how hideously clever the Communists were. Once they saw that no resistance would be offered by the Mandarin and his few soldiers they were polite in the extreme. They made many grand promises of reform. Every citizen would benefit from the paradise they promised, if only they would accept Communism.

But their politicking ended as the weather abruptly warmed. They could not risk being cut off from their stronghold to the northwest. They must get back across the frozen Yellow River before it became a raging torrent again.

"Praise God they are gone," Gladys told the Mandarin.

"We haven't seen the last of them, Ai-Weh-Deh. And

they won't be so polite when they are in control. They believe in exterminating all purveyors of the old way. Their cold-blooded economic theory—Communism is far too barren to be called a 'philosophy'—says that 'if the end is good *any* means to attain that end is justified.'"

Gladys had to brush this worry aside. She had her own ministry to occupy all her time and effort. And of course she took in more children. How could she refuse a small boy orphaned during another flood by the Yellow River? And the Mandarin himself placed an eight-year-old girl, Lan-Hsiang, with Gladys. This brought her family of children to five. Other orphans came and went but these five seemed truly Gladys's own.

By now Gladys knew China was her home. What greater commitment could she make to China than taking out citizenship? In 1936 she became a citizen. No one had better call her a foreign devil now.

"But I can't remember the last time anyone called me anything but Ai-Weh-Deh," she admitted.

In Tsechow, old Mrs. Smith had passed away. What a great friend she had been to Gladys. She had comforted her and counseled her during Jeannie's madness. Mrs. Smith had also sent Lu-Yung-Cheng to help at the mission, even paying his salary. More than anyone, even more than Jeannie Lawson, Mrs. Smith was her exemplar of a hard-working, commonsense missionary.

Soon Mrs. Smith was replaced by missionaries from Gladys's own generation. In fact David and Jean Davis were almost the same age as Gladys, both in their early thirties. David was a lean, long-faced Welshman. Jean was Scottish. They had a small bubbly son, Murray, who looked as if he could rival any child for mischief.

"You were turned down by the China Inland Mission?" David Davis said to Gladys in disbelief. "Because they didn't think you could master Chinese? I've never met anyone more articulate in the Shansi mountain dialects. You speak one *tu-hwa* after another, and so rapidly. And you're doing exactly what I want to do. Not that I'm criticizing Mrs. Smith in any way, God rest her brave soul. But I want to go into the mountain villages just as you have done! Our parish here covers five thousand square miles, you know."

Although David flattered Gladys for her fluent mountain dialects, he was an old China hand himself. He was as worried about the presence of Communists to the northwest as the Mandarin.

"They're ruthless, Ai-Weh-Deh," the Mandarin told Gladys. "They will kill any opposition in a split second. But they are a clever bunch, too. They're recruiting peasants for their army by promising them everything. What a pity. Chiang Kai-shek and his Nationalist government have already extended education, telephone service, rail service, even airplane service into many parts of China. But it isn't proceeding fast enough because the warlords resist. Chiang Kai-shek even approved land reform for the peasants. Every ten farm families is a *chia,* to be represented by one spokesman they themselves elect. Every ten *chias* is a *pao,* to be represented by one headman the spokesmen elect. The peasants are not only to own land but to have a voice in their government. But the warlords won't implement Chiang Kai-shek's land reforms or if they do they appoint their own spokesman. So the peasants are disillusioned and they turn to the Communists."

Before David Davis became a missionary he had worked as a customs inspector on the Yangtze River in south China. He had many run-ins with Communists there. He told Gladys of one such experience that changed his life. After he had seized weapons being shipped to local Communists, one evening the Communists kidnapped him. He was held in a house on a hill bordering the Yangtze River. He was to be executed at next light. He prayed for deliverance all night. That next dawn he watched in horror as another prisoner was beheaded. David's turn was next.

At that very moment the Communists spotted a British gunboat cruising up the Yangtze. David couldn't believe his captors were foolish enough to open fire on it. They were usually so cunning. But this time they were hot-tempered. Within minutes enormous shells from the gunboat began to burst around the house. In the mismatched fire fight that followed, David simply walked away from his captors. He couldn't believe they had not bound him. God had surely delivered him that morning. It was at that moment he dedicated the rest of his life to serving God.

"You were surely sent here by God," gasped Gladys. "And you do know the Communists, don't you?"

David Davis knew much about the Japanese problem too. Even Gladys knew how strong they were in the northeast. They occupied Manchuria—in fact they had renamed it Manchukuo. She also had heard rumors of how Japan had annexed part of Mongolia into Manchukuo in 1933 and demanded the "liberation" of five other northeastern Chinese provinces.

But she was not aware of how much the Japanese had made other inroads into China too. By an old treaty they were allowed, like several other foreign powers, to have troops in the Beijing area. This was an aftermath of the Boxer Rebellion in 1900. The troops were there to keep the trade corridor open from Beijing to the seaport of Tientsien. Gladys had never seen any foreign troops there when she first arrived in China, but David Davis said there were now about seven thousand Japanese soldiers in the corridor.

Further south the Japanese had troops in Shanghai. This presence stemmed from a supposed attack there on one Japanese seamen. After a fierce forty-day fight between Chinese and Japanese troops, the situation was resolved but Japanese troops were allowed to remain in that city. Any resistance from China anywhere brought an immediate and violent response from Japan.

"But can't the Japanese be stopped?" asked Gladys in dismay.

"Look at Chiang Kai-shek's dilemma. He has supreme authority only in the south. In the north where he must stop the Japanese he is also openly opposed by the Communists and obstructed behind his back by warlords."

In late 1936 the volatility of the situation was brought out starkly—not only for Gladys but for all of China. Chiang Kai-shek—called "Generalissimo" by friends and foes alike—had gone to Sian, less than two hundred miles west of Yangcheng. The Generalissimo was intending to motivate the local warlords and their troops to move against the Communists to the north around Yenan. The Communists there had built their remnant army up to a hundred thousand soldiers, some claimed.

But in Sian, Chiang Kai-shek was kidnapped by none other than Chang Hsueh-liang, the "Young Marshal" Gladys had learned about years before. The Young Marshal insisted the Nationalists give up their attempts to annihilate the Communists and unite against the Japanese. Chiang Kai-shek refused. The Communists had to be crushed, he insisted. They were a much greater threat to freedom than Japan.

There was an impasse. Day after day nothing happened. Soon the news of the kidnapping broke out.

"It seems Chiang Kai-shek is appreciated more than anyone realized," said David Davis to Gladys. "There is a genuine gloom over his capture. Without him China will fall apart and be conquered by the Japanese."

Finally, it was Chiang Kai-shek's wife who negotiated a truce. This fact was stunning in China where women were treated as little more than livestock.

Mayling was one of the three Soong sisters. All three had married powerful men. Chingling was the wife of Sun Yat-sen. Eling was the wife of a powerful financier, H. H. Kung.

Gladys was enthralled. Mayling was a Christian too. She supposedly had converted Chiang Kai-shek to Christianity. In spite of all the criticism piled on Chiang Kai-shek, none was aimed at personal vices. He didn't smoke, didn't drink, and didn't take other wives. When Mayling, or "Madam Chiang," finally negotiated his freedom genuine joy swept China. The Generalissimo was free!

"The Nationalists have arrested the Young Marshall," David Davis informed Gladys. "Is it possible Madam Chiang negotiated her husband's release without making concessions? Or did Madam Chiang have to agree that the Nationalists would no longer pursue the Communists?"

The Japanese may have well decided the Nationalists were going to make peace with the Communists so that united the two rivals could fight Japan. Because in July of 1937, Japan ignited the powder keg that was China.

eleven

July 1937 brought another incident of a Japanese supposedly accosted, this one at the Marco Polo Bridge fifteen miles from Beijing. Skirmishes between Japanese and Chinese troops broke out and spread. Within six days the seven thousand Japanese troops in the corridor had ballooned into twenty thousand. There was still a pretense of a fragile truce. But when the Communists pledged in September they would no longer try to overthrow the Nationalist government, and in fact they would join the Nationalist armies, everyone knew the Japanese would no longer be appeased. War had begun between Japan and China.

"Japan may have sealed our doom," lamented David Davis, "but not the way they think. Now the Communists can officially raise armies. When this war with Japan is all over the Communists will have an enormous army and it will be armed to the teeth!"

War was certainly no strategic problem for Japan, which

had already controlled northeast China for several years. They had stockpiled a magnificent war machine there, just waiting to be released. From there tanks and infantry began to conquer Chinese territory relentlessly, always preceded by the strafing and bombing of warplanes.

The Chinese had nothing to oppose Japan's air power. Beijing had fallen to them at the very outbreak of war. By the end of November the Japanese had complete control of Shanghai. Two weeks later the Nationalists' own headquarters in Nanjing was in the hands of the Japanese.

The Nationalists retreated far inland to set up headquarters in Chungking, about five hundred miles southwest of Yangcheng in the province of Szechuan.

One spring morning of 1938 Gladys was kneeling in prayer in an upstairs room at the Inn of Eight Happinesses. Yang was with her, as well as four other converts.

"I hear a peculiar buzzing noise!" said Yang, somewhat ashamed because he had to interrupt Gladys.

Gladys listened hard. "It's getting louder." The windows were not papered now that it was spring. Gladys rose to walk to a window. Everyone on the street below was looking up at the sky. "What do you see?" she yelled down.

"Beautiful silver birds!"

Suddenly there was a bone-rattling explosion. Another. Another. Bombs! War had come to Yangcheng! The street below was lost in a flash. The world fell away. Everything was black. Gladys heard the murmur of voices. There were no explosions now, only crushing weight on her back.

"They're under here!" someone screamed.

Commotion ensued. Finally the weight was off her back. Hands were turning her. She blinked at blue sky.

Faces ogled her. She groaned. She was lifted and carried somewhere.

Gradually she regained her senses. All who had been in the room with her were alive too. A bomb had struck the corner of the inn. Nine people out on the street had died. Gladys and the others had tumbled out of the disintegrating room to fall on other rubble below. Then they were covered by more cascading rubble. Gladys had been unconscious for some time.

"Help me up," she asked.

Upright, she brushed herself off. She was shaken, bruised, and scratched, but otherwise all right. She walked on wobbly legs to get her medicine kit. She had little more than wads of cotton, a can of borax powder for cleaning wounds, and a bottle of permanganate of potash for a disinfectant. She had Yang tear a sheet in strips for bandaging.

Then they went inside the wall at the East Gate to the main street of Yangcheng. Piles of rubble testified to the devastation. Dead people were everywhere. Wounded were groaning, some in sight, some covered by debris.

"We have no time to mourn," snapped Gladys.

She organized a brigade. Strong young men were to uncover the bodies. The wounded were to be carried inside any buildings still standing. The dead were to be carried outside the city walls. She and the women would do what nursing was possible. Water must be boiled.

She began to attend to the wounded. Borax powder and purple permanganate crystals were dissolved in separate containers of hot water. She could do little more than clean the wound, disinfect it, and bandage it. No stitching, no setting of broken bones. Not just yet. She must first stop

139

infection and bleeding.

More men were enlisted to clear a pathway through main street. All day long she and her helpers worked their way down the street.

"Two temples still stand!" boomed a familiar voice. The Town Crier was still alive. Over and over he chanted, "The Mandarin commands we take the homeless to the Temple of Lang Quai. The wounded we will tend in the Temple of Buddha."

By late afternoon Gladys and her helpers reached the yamen. The Mandarin was there with the jail warden and several other officials. With prisoners and many other helpers they had been doing the same chore as Gladys but from the other end of main street. The officials looked haggard, defeated. Their great city walls of interlocking stone were no defense against modern weapons.

"Still, there is much to be done in defeat too," said the Mandarin.

"And what of the Japanese?" asked one official. It was one question no one wanted to hear.

"The radio says their ground troops are already in Lu-an," answered the Mandarin in a very tired voice.

Lu-an was a mere sixty miles north! "We must not be here when the troops get here," declared Gladys.

"Yes," agreed the Mandarin. "We have a day or two to bury the dead and organize. Then we must go off into the remotest parts of the mountains."

They discussed the destinations of various groups from Yangcheng. The entire lot of survivors obviously could not inundate one mountain village. There had to be a plan. Eventually they reached agreement. It was decided Gladys and her converts, about forty in all, would trek to Bei Chai Chuang, a village hidden on the other side of a mountain, away from any mule trail.

With all the work that had to be done it seemed just a moment before departure was upon them. Tears blinded her as she said farewell to Yang, the loyal cook who had been a big part of her life for so many years. Yang had decided to return to his home village. The only thing worse than leaving Yang would have been to part with one of her five children.

"But, praise God, they are with me," she said as her group trudged reluctantly off toward Bei Chai Chuang.

They descended into a canyon, walked along a dry river bed for a mile or two, then ascended the mountainside to a high trail. Never had her recent injuries seemed so painful. Gladys was very badly bruised. But perhaps she had more injuries than that. How her knees throbbed.

Finally they simply left the trail to climb higher. There was no trail to Bei Chai Chung. It seemed to Gladys that once they topped the mountain and went down its hidden side Bei Chai Chuang might not even be there. But of course it was there. And, as tiny as it was, it was within walls. No outsider who had made such a trek needed to be told that the people who inhabited the eight houses there were fiercely independent!

"Things in the sky that drop death?" said one of the farmers after Gladys's group arrived. "How is that possible? Only birds fly." But in the days ahead this skeptic would walk to the crest of the mountain to see silvery planes cruising the valley below.

Only such a preposterous story could have made him

doubt Gladys. Because the Foot Inspector had been at Bei Chai Chuang too. The people of the tiny village liked Gladys and without hesitation welcomed the refugees. The life they led was simple but sufficient. They farmed tiny plots of millet, corn, and cotton. They tended pigs, sheep, cattle, and chickens. They trapped pheasants and rabbits. What else was needed?

"We have everything here. Why are you leaving?" one of villagers asked Gladys a week later.

"The others are staying. I must know what is happening down in Yangcheng."

"Yangcheng! Didn't you tell us the enemy was down there?"

"Perhaps they've moved on. We won't burden you any longer than necessary."

Gladys trudged up the mountain. Her knees began to throb painfully. Should she go back to Bei Chai Chuang? No, she had to see if Yangcheng was occupied. Once at the summit she felt better. The descent down the other side of the mountain was slow but less painful.

After many hours of steady walking, she approached Yangcheng. Nothing looked more deserted. Still she entered neither the West Gate nor the East Gate but crept cautiously to the Inn of Eight Happinesses.

There was no one in sight on the deserted street that fronted the inn. She entered her battered courtyard. Nothing. It was a cobbled ruin, just as she left it. What had she expected?

"The Japanese are here," said a voice behind her.

"What!"

She turned to see an old man, a Chinese whom she

knew was a water-carrier in Yangcheng. He did not have a good reputation. Why was he trying to scare her? What was he up to? Had he remained behind to loot? It seemed obvious he was lying. Did he want her to leave so he could rummage through her inn? *Well, welcome to it,* she thought. Nothing of any value was here. Only memories. She didn't want a conversation with the old man. In fact she wanted to get away from him, so she quietly slipped past him without speaking.

"Some people are not very grateful. . ." he muttered as she left.

This time she skirted the city wall to go to the West Gate. It was closer to where she would eventually have to descend to walk back to Bei Chai Chuang. Perhaps she would glance inside the city to see if there was any evidence the Japanese had ever been there. As she clambered along she remembered with disgust the old water carrier. Then she startled herself. What if he had been an enemy soldier? She could have been shot and never known what hit her. What if he had been a Chinese soldier? He too might have shot her—for a looter! She felt very foolish now as she stumbled along the great stone wall.

"Lord, protect me from my own foolishness," she whispered.

Suddenly there was an explosion!

Gladys dived to the ground. Planes again? Was it a bomb? With an effort she rolled over to gawk at the sky. She saw nothing. Pop. Pop. Pop. Where had she heard that peculiar firecracker sound before? Russia! It was gunfire. Rifles, no doubt. Another explosion! Poof! Another explosion. Buzzing. She looked at the sky. There was a plane! It careened down toward Yangcheng. Pop! Pop! Pop! Was someone firing at the plane? An enormous explosion shuddered through her. Oh, how her bones ached.

She scrambled away from the wall. What if the great stones fell on her? But she was becoming hysterical. She had to calm herself.

"Oh, sweet Jesus, deliver me from this battle," she prayed.

Calmed, she crept down the slope, through a graveyard, across the two-foot-high green stalks of a small wheat field. Only where the field stopped and the mountain slope took a sudden dip into a precipitous cliff did she look back.

Yes, she saw soldiers on the slope near the West Gate. They wore khaki uniforms and helmets. Japanese! Now on the wall she saw a blue-clad, cloth-capped soldier. He was a Chinese Nationalist soldier. He seemed woefully unprotected. He fired his rifle and ducked out of sight. Another Chinese soldier rose above the wall, fired his rifle, and ducked back. Would the Chinese soldiers be dead in a few hours? War was so sickening. *Oh Lord, their poor souls are not saved either.*

"Surely Satan dances in joy at such tragic sights," whispered Gladys.

She could do nothing. And getting captured would be monumentally stupid. But what was her best escape route? She realized now that during her arrival her stroll for a mile or two along the cobbly river bed at the canyon floor had been very foolish. In many places in the canyon the river was bounded by sheer walls; there was no quick way out. No, this time she would have to cross the canyon as quickly as possible, climb for a while, and take the very difficult slope trail above the canyon. It was much more tiring. And her knees and muscles were burning soreness now. But she had no choice. She couldn't take the chance of meeting Japanese soldiers on the canyon floor.

After her descent, she crouched in the bushes, studying the canyon. "I'll dash across the river and climb as fast as I can."

Glancing up she saw the steep climb that awaited her. She couldn't even see the high trail. *Good,* she thought, refusing to think of the pain it would cost her, *the Japanese soldiers won't see it either.* Taking a hard look down the canyon, reassuring herself no one was coming, she stumbled gimpy-legged across the river bed.

She collapsed in the brush, resting for a few moments, then clambered up the side. Climbing was murderous to her now. But she didn't stop until she fell onto the high trail, having managed the last few yards only by clawing ahead on her hands and knees.

"Praise You, God," she gasped.

She rolled over to survey the canyon floor. Her heart almost stopped. Clattering down the river bed was a small army. Mules with heavy packs. Mules pulling small cannons. And khaki-uniformed soldiers on foot. Perhaps five hundred of them. The Japanese soldiers already at Yangcheng must have been only a reconnaissance squad. Gladys couldn't know how many Nationalist soldiers defended Yangcheng, but she was sure they weren't numerous enough to hold out against these reinforcements coming along the canyon floor with their cannons. But even this force wouldn't be used until the Chinese defenders had been devastated by the dive bombers.

"Lord, have mercy on all these innocents," prayed Gladys.

It was fast getting dark now. She would never reach Bei Chai Chuang this night. It was too dangerous to walk the trail in the dark. She would just have to curl up and go to sleep. There were many stories of wolves in these mountains. *Well, let them come,* she thought angrily. *I'm hungry enough to eat one.* Then Gladys shuddered. What if the night sky brought one of those freaky spring storms that threw down hail or even sleet? She was no match for that. Her foolishness this day topped just about anything she had done before. From now on a man of her party could reconnoiter. The Chinese mountain men were more cunning at these things than she was anyway. They were unforgiving too. She pitied Japanese soldiers who were foolish enough to wander off from the main force into the high mountains. But how could she be thinking of pity for these invaders?

"Because of the love of Christ," she answered herself, just before she fell asleep.

The next morning Gladys limped on until she reached Bei Chai Chuang. One day not much later one of the scouts came back with good news. The Japanese had abandoned Yangcheng. What good did it do their conquest of all of China to keep precious soldiers posted in a deserted town? But was it a trick? No, said the scouts, the Town Crier was announcing outside the city gates that the Mandarin declared Yangcheng safe again. So Gladys and a handful of her group returned to Yangcheng. The others remained behind, among them ten who were recovering from serious wounds.

But tragedy awaited in Yangcheng. Many of the inhabitants—foolish like Gladys but not so lucky—had come back too soon. The Japanese had still been there, very angry over resistance from the Nationalist soldiers. The Japanese had lost several of their soldiers. So as the inhabitants naively wandered back into the city too soon, they were executed. Their lifeless bodies were stacked everywhere. Men, women, and children, a blanket execution.

"It appears the Japanese bayoneted them," said the Mandarin, never looking more depressed, "so they wouldn't waste bullets."

"Now we really know the evil that threatens us," mumbled Gladys. "The Japanese murder all Chinese."

There could be no delusion now about cooperating with the Japanese as if they might prove benefactors. The residents had dug a huge pit for the dead outside the city walls after the first time Yangcheng was bombed. Now the pit was extended. The carnage was even worse than it first appeared.

Back in the courtyard of the Inn of Eight Happinesses, Gladys found three more dead Chinese. She made sure these, too, were buried. What had they been doing there? Looking for a place to rest? Was there no end to this killing? Where were the Japanese now? In Tsechow? She suddenly remembered the Davises! She said a prayer for them. Doubt and fear were crushing her. Might not Japanese patrols return to Yangcheng periodically? To kill again? To maintain a reign of terror? How could the Mandarin think they would simply resume their lives again?

"I've been very foolish, Lord, and You have protected me. But from this time on, although I will be as harmless as a dove I will also be as wise as a serpent."

Extremely depressed, she left the inn and headed back to Bei Chai Chuang. Gladys no longer regarded Bei Chai Chuang as some temporary stopover. It wasn't fair to her group. It wasn't fair for the villagers. Her group had been crammed inside their eight houses. That imposition on them must stop.

The villagers tactfully suggested a cave. Like many caves in these mountain provinces it was no simple hole in the wall. The inside had been carefully sculpted into a large arched room and supported. The opening was walled off with stone. In the stone wall was a very large doorway, because the villagers used this particular cave to shelter their livestock in bad weather. But they would not need the cave for another several months. So Gladys and her group cleaned it out and moved in. Word spread among the mountain people that a "hospital" existed in Bei Chai Chuang. Wounded Chinese began to straggle in.

"Welcome, friend," Gladys would say without fail before she began her very limited medical treatment.

If a man were gunshot, she would clean his wound, often squirting the solution containing permanganate of potash into a deep hole with a syringe she had. She splinted broken bones too. Internal injuries were another matter. She could do very little but offer rest. And a gunshot wound to the stomach was slow death to the victim.

One of the refugees was none other than Hsi-Lien, the inn's very first muleteer. And a Christian.

"Hsi-Lien," she gasped, "you look very sick."

"My heart has been torn out of me."

"But what do you mean?"

"The Japanese came to Tsechow. They insisted I use my mule train to transport ammunition for them. I refused. I could not carry bullets that killed people."

Then Hsi-Lien broke down. It was only after hours of comforting him that Gladys learned the horror that tormented him. The Japanese had punished him by locking his wife and three children inside his house. He himself was tied outside. Then soldiers torched the house. All Hsi-Lien could do was to try to drown out the screams of his wife and children with screams of his own.

"Will this pain in my heart ever cease?" he asked Gladys.

Gladys remembered the Fourteenth Chapter of the Book of John. "Our Savior said 'Let not your heart be troubled: ye believe in God, believe also in me. In my Father's house are many mansions: if it were not so, I would have told you. I go to prepare a place for you. And if I go and prepare a place for you, I will come again, and receive you unto myself; that where I am, there ye may be also.' And there now in that mansion in paradise, Hsi-Lien, are your wife and children. So let not your heart be troubled."

But Gladys herself was very troubled. The Japanese were monsters without equal. How could she love such people? How could she turn her other cheek? Their absolute cruelty was tearing away her beliefs almost as surely as their bullets tore away flesh.

After a few weeks in Bei Chai Chuang she cautiously returned to Yangcheng, watching the green slopes and the blue sky. All the mountain people watched the sky for planes now, because the Japanese scouted that way. And no one wanted to be the one who divulged the location of a hideout.

She was happy to see her old friend, the Mandarin. *"Chi-la fan ma?"* she greeted him.

After several minutes of the required civility, the Mandarin said, "The enemy has evacuated Tsechow. They have pulled back to Lu-an. They don't want to be overextended when winter comes." But he seemed gloomy nevertheless.

"Your Eminence may be holding back bad news," she said softly.

"Where do I start, Ai-Weh-Deh? With the general? Or the specific?"

"As your Eminence wishes."

"Your convert Hsi-Lien was tormented in the cruelest way by the Japanese in Tsechow."

"Yes, I know of his tragedy. I appreciate your concern." Gladys had always suspected the Mandarin was tender-hearted for all people, great and small. But the story of Hsi-Lien seemed especially troubling to him. "What of the more general news, your Eminence?"

"I now see the collapse of China. That depresses me as I have never been depressed before. Either the Japanese will win—and you have seen what devils they are—or eventually the Communists will win—and you know what devils they are. You told me how the Communists tried to execute your friend David Davis."

With the Japanese temporarily idle, Gladys began to visit Yangcheng more and more. Of course her job as Foot Inspector was suspended indefinitely. But she still visited villages because she had to tend her flocks. She had Christian converts scattered in many villages now.

The Inn of Eight Happinesses lay in ruins and dormant. Restoration seemed futile. The mule trains could no longer get past Lu-an, so that trafficking virtually stopped.

Yang had never returned to Yangcheng from his home village. Because his home village was beyond the Mandarin's domain, Gladys had little chance of ever visiting it. She had to enlist all the hope of a Christian not to worry more and more about Yang's fate. Could he have suffered under the Japanese like Hsi-Lien? Faithful Yang would never deny his belief either.

twelve

Springtime brought the Japanese war machine again. Once again the local Chinese planned how they would hide in distant mountain villages until the Japanese left at summer's end. But this time the Nationalist authorities brought them to their knees.

"Burn all the crops?" questioned the Mandarin in Gladys's presence. "Rip off all the roofs of our buildings?"

"No food, no shelter," murmured Gladys, but not in appreciation.

"These are wise stratagems of war perhaps," said the Mandarin, his face ashen. "Our High Command says we can exist in the remote villages. The Japanese are afraid to venture off into the high mountains. Anyway, we have no choice. But must we also tear off the roof of the Pagoda of the Scorpion?"

The Pagoda of the Scorpion was very ancient, supposedly built around a sleeping scorpion to permanently imprison it. The scorpion was a giant that would like nothing more than to ravage the countryside once again. Destroying the roof would release the monster.

"Perhaps you should destroy the roof anyway, Eminence," advised Gladys, who considered that pagoda a pagan eyesore.

"But who will do it? Where can I find someone who does not believe the legend?"

"Perhaps a group of Christians?"

"What an excellent idea," he replied.

So Gladys enlisted several Christian men to remove the roof from the pagoda. Not long after that event, Gladys was invited to a banquet given by the Mandarin. For a while now she had been his guest at special occasions if she were in Yangcheng. She was usually the only woman present.

"Tsing tsoa, Ai-Weh-Deh," said the Mandarin, waving to a place to his right. "Closer, closer," he coaxed her as she tried to decide just where to sit.

"Your Eminence doesn't mean? . . ."

"Tsing tsoa," he insisted. "Here on my right side."

Immediately to the Mandarin's right was the seat of honor. Gladys was startled. What could it mean? The warden of the jail was there. So were the Mandarin's other officials and several wealthy merchants. Toward the end of the banquet the Mandarin stood and spoke. Gladys was startled when he began speaking about her.

Yes, he said, from the other side of the world Ai-Weh-Deh journeyed to China, owing allegiance only to her Living God. She had brought her Christianity to Yangcheng. No, she had not sat hidden inside a temple contemplating how virtuous she was. She had unbound the feet of infants. She had helped the poor. She had visited the jails. She had taken orphans under her roof. She had nursed the wounded. Her faith was alive. More than anyone the Mandarin had ever met, Ai-Weh-Deh demonstrated the power of love. She loved China so much she became a citizen. And more than any man he had ever met, the simple muleteer Hsi-Lien demonstrated the power of love. The Mandarin admitted he had debated with her the merits of her faith against the merits of his old Confucius ways a hundred times.

"But Confucianism lives in my head," he declared, "not in my heart, as Christianity does in Ai-Weh-Deh and her converts." Then he concluded, "I wish to become a Christian!"

Gladys was stunned! Her head was buzzing. What a surprise. She realized the group was expecting her to say something. She rose and thanked the Mandarin for praising her. Then she congratulated him for making a decision that would save him for eternity. She sat down. She could not improve on what the Mandarin had already said.

"Now we must discuss our plans for evacuation," said the Mandarin.

The warden of the jail had a problem. He grumbled, "The last time we evacuated Yangcheng I had a terrible time leading shackled prisoners through the mountains, then finding them shelter, then feeding them."

"Why not take an alternative that is much safer and much cheaper?" asked a merchant matter-of-factly. "Execute them."

"No!" interrupted Gladys, "your Eminence, you must not allow that." The Mandarin looked at her expectantly. Gladys continued, "Release them to the custody of relatives

154

or friends. Make the custodians pay a small fee to show their good faith."

Even the merchant appreciated that. "A small fee for a worthless prisoner? Excellent idea."

And the Mandarin agreed. The next day the Town Crier spread the decree. All prisoners had to be claimed by a relative or friend who would accept responsibility for their behavior while in custody and also for their return. In addition, a small fee would be charged. Any prisoners not claimed would be beheaded! This latter stipulation worried Gladys.

But she had many things to do before she departed to Bei Chai Chuang. Not the least of her last-minute duties was to instruct the Mandarin as a new Christian. This was not difficult because she had discussed many attributes of Christianity with him before. Soon she was satisfied he would leave for his hideout well-armored in Christ.

As the deadline for the end of the claiming period for the prisoners approached, she visited the jail.

"Twelve have not been claimed, Ai-Weh-Deh," admitted the warden.

Two Gladys knew very well. One was Feng, the Buddhist priest the prisoners accepted as their leader. The other was an educated but corrupt businessman named Sheng-Li. Sheng-Li had forged the "chop," the stone seal that identified a businessman's papers, to make a tidy living for himself until he was caught. But Sheng-Li was so bubbly and pleasant he disarmed even Gladys. She would never be able to live with herself if these two capable but flawed men were executed.

"Release Sheng-Li and Feng to me," she told the warden.

"There are ten more," he prompted.

"Surely their relatives will come for them at the last moment," she said optimistically after taking custody of Feng and Sheng-Li.

But she returned to the jail the day before any remaining prisoners were to be executed. Eight were left. She was allowed to question them individually. They all told the same story.

"I have relatives who would take me," they said sorrowfully, "but there is not enough time for the news to travel there and for them to come for me. Don't you see? It's so unfair."

But although their stories were the same, their crimes were certainly not the same. Two were murderers. And what of the fees? As trifling as the fee was, the sum was beyond Gladys's means. Gladys had to withdraw and pray. Should she take murderers with her to Bei Chai Chuang? Would God protect her and her group?

Her God was merciful. She felt God was surely saying to her "Show mercy." She returned to the warden. "These men claim their relatives will eventually take responsibility for them. Can I send you the fees I get from the relatives later?"

"That's a great deal to ask," he muttered.

But Gladys could tell the warden was only too happy to have the issue of the prisoners resolved. "No more prisoners!" his face seemed to beam after he agreed to her proposal. He seemed in flight to his hideout already.

Everyone was anxious to leave. The weather was warm, and who knew when the Japanese troops would once again come rumbling down the river bed in the canyon floor below? Their extreme brutality to which they often devilishly added the most inhuman cruelties was well established by now. They tortured as a matter of course. Many a Chinese had suffered torn ligaments or fractured bones or the loss of teeth—for no discernible offense at all. No Chinese wanted to encounter the Japanese. So Yangcheng in ruins, fields of millet and spring corn flaming behind them, all the Chinese left for their hideaways.

"And it's off to Bei Chai Chuang for us," Gladys said as she trudged off with her converts and ten prisoners.

Shortly after their arrival in Bei Chai Chuang, she got word one of her converts in a tiny village near the larger settlement of Chin Shui had been beaten by bandits. So she trudged for two and a half days through the mountains to nurse the man.

Word came to her there the Japanese had indeed taken Yangcheng again. Chin Shui was next in line. Gladys had started a small mission there. Immediately she left for Chin Shui to make sure her converts had hideaways to flee to. Japanese dive bombers were raining bombs on the village as she approached. Then the wings of death departed. Japanese ground troops would soon follow.

"We must leave Chin Shui in the next few hours," she told the people in her mission.

Making sure each one of her charges at the Mission had a place to go, she departed Chin Shui from its East Gate. A young woman named Wan Yu and a boy would accompany her to Bei Chai Chuang.

They had an open space of two miles to cross before ascending into the safety of the heights. The open space stopped Gladys in her tracks. A feeling of doom draped over the open space like a shroud. An encounter with Japanese in the open was certain death. God was surely telling her not to go, because on her way into Chin Shui she had felt nothing as she crossed that open space. Abruptly the three returned to Chin Shui and left by its West Gate. Many refugees were fleeing from that gate too.

Pop. Pop. Pop.

"God truly warned us," said Gladys upon hearing the distant gunfire.

Within minutes everyone was fleeing only from the West Gate because Japanese troops were now crossing the open space in front of the East Gate. They were firing on fleeing Chinese.

"Follow me," said Wan Yu forcefully. Gladys and the boy followed her through the chest-deep Chin River and up a small valley. There was no marked trail. Up the valley they trekked, past one tiny village after another. The sixth one, almost on the crest of the mountain, was Wan Yu's village. The three joined Wan Yu's mother, her brother, and his wife in the family home. Other refugees had come this far too. Soon Wan Yu's village, so pleasant among fields of millet and corn, accommodated many refugees, from the elderly and blind, to the tiniest infants.

"We're here until the Japanese pull back again," realized Gladys. "I see no way out. Please, God, don't let the Japanese reach us here before the air turns cold again."

But after about five weeks Gladys watched in horror as Japanese soldiers tromped up the valley and stopped to investigate a temple only fifty yards down the slope. Never had she believed they would come this far up such a remote valley. Chinese guerrillas were residing in the village too.

Fighting would be fierce.

The horns and drums of the priests at the temple carried across the mountain air. "The priests are summoning the Creator to protect the village," whispered Wan Yu.

"So must we," answered Gladys. So they all prayed. Miraculously the Japanese soldiers walked out of the temple and marched back down the valley. Not one shot had been fired.

Several weeks later the word came to Gladys that the Japanese had pulled back for the winter, not this time to Lu-an but only to Tsechow. That was very bad news, for David Davis and the Mission there. Gladys returned to Yangcheng to stay at the Inn of Eight Happinesses. A few mule trains even straggled in.

"It would almost be like old times if Yang were here," reflected Gladys sadly.

But Yang did not return. Rumors came in that he was dead. Had he been shot for Christ? He was at an age, however, when a natural cause could have ended his life. Gladys was not able to find out what happened.

By February 1939, she become so concerned about David Davis and his Mission that she slipped down into Tsechow, occupied by Japanese or not. She did not have to take the risk of entering the well-guarded gates of the city. The Mission, like her own in Yangcheng, lay outside the city walls.

"Gladys!" exclaimed David Davis. "Praise God, you're alive."

"It seems rather peaceful here," said Gladys, pleased.

"Calm before the storm, I fear," whispered David Davis. He told Gladys the guerrillas in the area had been joined by Chinese Nationalist soldiers, who adapted the same guer-rilla tactics of harassing the Japanese. Chinese Communist soldiers were also in the area, but as likely to shoot a Nationalist soldier as a Japanese soldier. Gladys already knew all this. But she had not extrapolated this information as far as David Davis had.

"The more the Japanese soldiers get shot at, the more brutal they will become to us here in Tsechow."

And as the Japanese patrols were sniped at more and more, their restraint in Tsechow grew less and less. Patrolling was so hazardous, their commanders felt com-pelled to indulge the soldiers when they returned. It became common to allow the soldiers to get drunk on rice wine and to commit any act, as long as it was not against another Japanese.

At the Mission, men and women were segregated into different living quarters. One night Gladys awakened to shouts and screams. She burst out of her room. The court-yard was full of Japanese soldiers. Their voices were loud, rasping, full of stupidity. They were drunk. They wanted women.

"Get out of here, you devils!" screamed Gladys.

A soldier slammed his rifle butt into the side of her head. No, she mustn't go down! One of the pet cruelties of the Japanese was to kick people to death. But Gladys did go down. A boot thumped into her ribs.

The next thing she knew Jean Davis was staring into her face with great concern. "Praise God you're alive," murmured Jean. Gladys blacked out again.

When she again awakened, Jean Davis said, "Relax, the Japanese are gone."

Slowly Gladys regained her senses. The women were safe. David Davis had arrived after Gladys had been knocked out. The women dragged into the courtyard by the drunken soldiers had fallen to their knees at David's command. They all started praying. Somehow God made the terrible shame of what the Japanese soldiers were about to do sink into their drunken consciences. Miraculously they departed without raping one woman. But David Davis had paid a price. His face was battered and ripped.

"He is being stitched up by a doctor," said Jean Davis.

Gladys's wounds were not as obvious. She had a very sore welt on the side of her head, but she hurt all over, the worst of the pain deep inside. She remembered now the soldiers kicking her. Perhaps they had fractured some ribs. She had nursed enough wounded people to know all the possibilities. A broken rib could puncture a lung. Or she might be bleeding from another internal organ.

After all her narrow escapes from the Japanese she had finally suffered their blows. Well, she was in God's hands now. He would either allow her to continue His work. Or He had another plan for her. She was nothing but His instrument. She would pray for the quick recovery of David Davis though.

"He has much work to do too, Lord," she prayed. Both she and David Davis recovered.

Two of the older missionaries had begged Davis to take them down to Chifu on the coast. There they could get passage back to England. So Davis agreed. The trip to Chifu and back would take one month. Before he left on his trip to Chifu, he reminded Gladys he wished his Mission in Tsechow to stay neutral. No matter how much she was tempted to help the official Chinese she must not help them in her capacity at his Mission.

She soon forgot this restriction in the flurry of activity the Mission required. She had to help with refugees, both adults and their children, as well as over a hundred orphans. Besides that, the Japanese abruptly retreated from Tsechow to Lu-an. Winter once again belonged to the Chinese soldiers!

Some Nationalist officers came to see Gladys. "We are so sorry to trouble you," said one man, stepping forward. He was very neat and handsome. He was also very disarming. Gladys could remember no one but the Mandarin who was so quiet-spoken, so well-mannered. The man continued, "I am Colonel Linnan, of the Intelligence Service."

"What do you want?" she asked, suspecting she would have to refuse. David Davis wanted the Mission to remain neutral.

"We wish only to board some Nationalist officers here," he said calmly. "Tsechow has limited facilities."

"But I cannot help you," Gladys said rudely. "The Mission must remain neutral."

Colonel Linnan said softly, "Chiang Kai-shek told us Christians would help us fight this terrible evil."

"The Generalissimo?" She was flabbergasted. If these men had come from the great warlord of Shansi, Yen Hsi-shan, she would have been stunned. But the Generalissimo? The most powerful man in China? Could they be telling her the truth? How could she turn them away? After all, David Davis had talked to the Japanese officials, hadn't he? "Come in and be seated," she said.

But the topic of conversation was direct. "Won't you help China?" asked Colonel Linnan.

"We can't board any of your men," she answered. "We must remain neutral. Don't you see these poor Chinese will lose their last refuge if we take sides?"

"Perhaps you can help us another way," suggested Colonel Linnan politely.

"I *am* Chinese," said Gladys, startling herself.

"Chinese!" he seemed delighted. "Well, perhaps we can talk later about how you might be able to help us."

He bowed politely and excused himself.

He did return. He discussed good and evil with Gladys. Yes, he was very much like the Mandarin. Very gentle. Very refined. It was plain he saw the Nationalists as a force for the good and the Japanese as a force of evil. If only she knew how difficult it was to accomplish change in China, he said. Chiang Kai-shek was a very good man, a frugal, faithful man, he insisted. A Christian married to a Christian wife. Many improvements had not been made by his Nationalist government but it was not because Chiang Kai-shek did not want to make the improvements. It was because the changes were resisted by the old traditionalists. And then just when Chiang Kai-shek seemed be making progress with his improvements the Japanese had invaded.

"Perhaps they invaded for that very reason," he said logically. "Once Chiang Kai-shek unites and improves China, we will be a nation that cannot be conquered."

Gladys was very impressed by his zeal. Yes, this was the reason and the compassion she wished to see combined in modern China. Yes, a modern China led by a compassionate Christian. If only Colonel Linnan were a Christian too. But what was she thinking?

Suddenly she realized she was quite infatuated by

Colonel Linnan. When had she ever felt so strongly about a man? Never. Did she dare hope he felt that way about her? He was about her same age. He was educated at Chiang Kai-shek's Central Military Academy in Nanjing. To Gladys he spoke perfect Mandarin. Although he was invariably polite he was also direct. He seemed never to lose his poise, except once. . .

"You are off to remote mountain villages?" he asked, somewhat amazed.

"I have started some missions there," she explained.

"But are you going on foot?"

"Yes, and alone."

"Alone! But bandits are in the mountains."

"They never bother me."

"Your God is powerful, but what if you fell and broke an ankle? Yes, what then? It happens." He looked sick.

His worried face was the most wonderful sight she had seen in a long time. Yes, she was sure now he cared for her. Besides, he visited her so frequently now, on the flimsiest of pretexts. She even walked with him inside the city. They strolled past the yamen, the temples, the bazaars. Everywhere people stopped to gawk in surprise. What a spectacle they must have been. A Nationalist Colonel and tiny Ai-Weh-Deh. And just before she left for the mountains he once again treated her to a very worried look.

"I won't be able to relax until you return," he admitted.

"He makes my heart sing," she admitted to herself later.

She wrote her parents a letter, preparing them for the possibility of her marriage to a Chinese Colonel. Then she went up into the mountains full of joy.

thirteen

Colonel Linnan was certainly present in her heart now. Never had Gladys felt so bonded to China, even if in her travels in the mountains now she saw soldiers of all persuasions: Nationalists and too often Communists and even Japanese.

On one of her trips into the mountains she met General Ley. She had heard rumors of this guerrilla commander. The rumors seemed too far-fetched to be true.

"So you are Ai-Weh-Deh?" he said. Gladys could scarcely believe her eyes. The sturdy man in front of her had short blonde hair. Her disbelief was not lost on General Ley. "Yes, I am European. And I was a Catholic priest, just as the gossips say."

"But a priest. . ."

"Japan enslaves its captives. They have made serfs out of all Koreans. They will make serfs out of all Chinese. They must be stopped—just as surely as the lunatic Hitler must be stopped in Europe. The force of evil in the world has never been more threatening than it is now."

"But to kill. . ."

"My dilemma is no different than any one else in the history of the human race: 'Is it right to oppose evil by force?' " General Ley expounded on the problem for a long time with Gladys. He finally realized she was not convinced. "Well, I feel better now anyway," he said with a smile. "My religion puts much stock in confession."

And he departed. Had she helped him in his dilemma? Perhaps, but only because she was someone—the Virtuous One—who heard his confession. She herself could not condone killing, even in defense.

But just where did she draw the line? Surely she was justified in helping refugees flee Japanese tyranny. But to what degree could a Christian resist evil?

When she returned to Tsechow she was overjoyed to see Colonel Linnan. She still could not resist triggering his concern. "I often see Japanese troops when I travel," she admitted.

"So dangerous!" he objected.

"They never bother me. I guess I look very harmless."

"They truly take no note of you?" Colonel Linnan's mind was racing. "It would be most helpful to China if we knew the locations of any advance scouting parties. Or any troop movements."

When he returned next he had a letter he wanted Gladys to carry. It was virtually official sanction from a Nationalist General for Gladys to "scout." Implied in that was her authority to direct Chinese troops to Japanese encampments. *Good Lord,* she thought, *will it ever come to that?* But from then on, Gladys did in fact report all

166

Japanese activity she saw in the mountains to the Chinese Nationalists.

One day in Tsechow a reporter from some American magazine called *Time* came to the Mission and interviewed her. Yes, she had witnessed the brutality of the Japanese troops on several occasions, she told him. And yes, she might have told the Chinese Nationalists.

"As a representative of this Mission I am neutral," she told him. "But I'm certainly not going to make excuses for the activities of the Japanese. Nor am I going to remain silent as to their movements."

War seemed a never-ending nightmare for Gladys. How many years had this insanity been going on now? The Japanese launched a strong offensive again in late spring. Gladys was nearly caught in the city of Lingchuang. Once again she was stumbling out of a city in a flood of refugees toward the remote mountains. This time dozens of Nationalist cavalry thundered past them. Oh, how noble they looked!

Then out of the blue screamed warplanes. Gladys dived behind an old stone wall. For long minutes the air popped with gunfire. The warplanes buzzed over again and again, raining bullets into them. Horses whinnied and screamed.

When it was silent again Gladys was witness to another tragedy of war. Cavalry—horses and riders—had been slaughtered. Killed with them were hundreds of refugees caught in the open. Babies, pregnant women. No innocents were spared. After many hours of helping the wounded, the surviving refugees trudged off once again into the mountains.

"Do not forsake us, Lord," Gladys prayed.

167

Again Gladys lived in a cave. Again survival was everything. The war seemed more hellish with every passing day. This time their cave was so remote the nearest source of water was five miles away. And yet once again when the Japanese pulled back she went down into Tsechow.

Her resolve remained. But how much bloodshed could one person witness—especially the blood of innocents—and keep the faith? Even Colonel Linnan's proposal of marriage, which she had longed for, could barely lift her spirits. In her exhaustion it seemed remote, dream-like. And he wanted her to become his bride as soon as possible, she suspected, so he would insist on whisking her out of harm's way. This she could not do. There were two hundred orphans at the Mission in Tsechow, including her own precious children. She would never leave them until they were all safe.

"They are my highest priority," she told Colonel Linnan. "All else must wait."

Something had to be done before the next great spring offensive by the Japanese. Because once again it would bring heartbreak. And how many chances to escape death would her two hundred young charges get?

A plea by letter to Madam Chiang Kai-shek brought good news. Yes, the orphans could be brought to Sian, where they would be cared for, far west of the Japanese threat. Gladys planned their flight. They had to be walked south to the Yellow River. There they could be ferried across the vast river. Then a train would take them west to Sian. But they must accomplish it before the Japanese returned.

In early 1940, one of her helpers, Tsin Pen Kuang, left Tsechow with half the orphan children. Many weeks later

Gladys learned the children reached Sian safely. But then she learned Tsin Pen Kuang had been captured by the Japanese trying to return to Tsechow. *Oh, Lord, what is the fate of this faithful man? And what will become of the children still in Tsechow?* For she had just heard the Japanese had started their spring offensive.

After much prayer, Gladys told David Davis, "I must move all the orphans to Yangcheng. Often the Japanese don't go on to Yangcheng."

"I agree," he said. "The Japanese get more brutal with each occupation."

So her helpers shepherded the children up the heights to Yangcheng. Gladys remained in Tsechow. Nearly one thousand other refugees were still at the Mission. She had to help David Davis arrange their plans of flight. But one afternoon Davis told her the Japanese were one day away from Tsechow. Perhaps less. Gladys must leave. The orphans awaited her in Yangcheng.

Still, she wasn't going to panic for her own safety. If the Japanese arrived before she was able to depart she would just slip away later. She had survived their occupation before.

Her activity was interrupted by an orderly from a Nationalist General. He offered her safe conduct with the Nationalist army as it retreated into safe territory.

"Oh, but I must join my orphans in Yangcheng."

"All of the province of Shansi is going to be very dangerous for you now. There is a price on your head."

"I don't believe you," she said bluntly.

"Read this handbill the Japanese are posting north of here." He thrust a sheet of paper at her and added, "Soon they will posting it all over this area too."

Gladys read the handbill. Yes, there was a reward for the Mandarin. There was a reward for a well-know patriot of Tsechow as well. And there was a reward for a spy: "the small woman known as Ai-Weh-Deh"!

"Who betrayed me?" she blurted.

"Get out of Tsechow!" warned the orderly.

Yes, *Flee, save your lives, and be like the heath in the wilderness,* screamed the prophet Jeremiah from her memory of the Bible. Now Gladys was numb with dread. The handbill was her death warrant. Had she waited too long? She shooed the orderly away. She had to get to Yangcheng. She gathered her few belongings. Before she left she burned her correspondence. There had been a letter from her parents saying it was fine with them if she wanted to marry the Chinese Colonel. Nothing must be left for the Japanese. She was a pariah. Had it been the reporter from the American magazine *Time* who exposed her? Perhaps. In the magazine? In a letter? In a conversation? What did it matter? She toiled all night long. It was dawn by the time she was ready to flee. She hurriedly told a very groggy David Davis she was leaving.

"The Japanese are entering the city!" someone screamed.

The Mission lay outside the city walls. Gladys dashed out the back gate of the Mission into a cemetery. To her horror she saw a long line of marching soldiers only about one hundred yards away. Bullets sang past her. An old moat lay ahead of her. If only she could reach it. Something whomped her in the back. The next thing she knew she was flat on her face. But not dead, only terrified. Clutching her bundle, she crawled into the moat, bullets

170

whining all around her. Once in the moat she crouched down and stumbled toward a cornfield.

She wormed into the cover of tall stalks. Only in the middle of the field did she pause to inspect herself. Her fingers probed a stinging area of her right shoulder. There was very little blood. A bullet must have made the shallowest furrow in her flesh.

"Thank You, God, for protecting me," she prayed, "Now please make the soldiers forget me."

And the soldiers apparently did forget her. They had more important prey to press. She could well imagine a brutal Japanese soldier being severely reprimanded by an even more brutal Japanese officer for chasing a small mousy woman into a corn field. But of course they did not know the small woman was the very important prey on their handbill! Still, she waited until dark to begin the journey to Yangcheng that she had made so many years before in a mule shanza.

Yes, ten years before. Or was it eleven? The ebb and flow of the war had robbed her of her calendar. Alive or dead seemed the only choices that mattered. She was not yet forty years old. She was sure of that. She felt disoriented. But she must not stop. For she had already made up her mind that she would take the children to Sian. She was not going to stay in Shansi. Her wonderful anonymity was gone, and summer was so dangerous. The Japanese were very active. Not to mention a Chinese Communist would be more than happy to shoot her for a reward.

"How much food do you have?" asked the very concerned Mandarin in Yangcheng two days later.

"Whatever you give us, Eminence."

"Us?"

171

"I'm taking the orphans with me."

"But aren't there several dozen, Ai-Weh-Deh?"

"About one hundred."

"One hundred! But you must cross mountains. You must cross the Yellow River. . . ."

"And if I stay?"

He frowned. "I'll give you sacks of millet. Some of my men can help you as far as the Yellow River. After that I can help you only with prayers."

"And I will pray for you, Eminence."

Gladys left, knowing that the Mandarin had a price on his head too. She might be able to flee Shansi. But he could not leave his duty. His only hope was that the Nationalists would eventually prevail against the Japanese, and after that the Nationalists must prevail against the Communists. Because either the Japanese or the Communists would execute him. During all that ebb and flow of battle he must never be caught. So why should she think her trek with the children was such an impossible task?

"Tomorrow we are going for a long walk in the mountains," she told the orphans at the inn. "At dawn you will roll your chopsticks and bowl up inside your bedding. Get a good night's sleep."

Although Gladys chose to avoid established trails the first part of their trek was not difficult for these children. It spoke of the harsh reality of China that the seventy children aged four to eight had taken many arduous journeys. So had the older seven boys and twenty girls. One of the oldest was Sualan, a slave girl being groomed for the harem of the Mandarin before Gladys's intervention. Among the children of course were Gladys's own two girls Ninepence and

Lan-Hsiang, as well as Less and her other two boys.

For lunch the caravan stopped by a stream to boil some millet. That evening the children slept in a remote Buddhist temple. The next night they were not so lucky. They huddled under their quilts in the cold mountain night. The third night they were in a village.

"How many days will it take to reach the Yellow River?" Ninepence asked Gladys discreetly.

"The mule trains take five days to make the journey," answered Gladys perkily.

But mules walked much faster and steadier than four-year-olds. And the mule trains used the main trail. Gladys had to avoid the main trail. Day after day the chattery, fidgety caravan followed the grain of the ridges and valleys to the southwest. The older boys were helpful to Gladys. Toward the end of the day they often carried the youngest ones on their backs. Where did they find such strength in their small bowls of millet? The Mandarin's men could not help with the children because they were loaded down with sacks of millet. The oldest girls were the most helpless of all. Their feet, once bound, were weak and crippled. And their skin seemed to burn and chap more easily.

Gladys could scarcely keep from crying when she examined her entourage. The four-year-olds had never known any life other than this one of fleeing and hunkering down. What cruelty mankind had dealt these shabbily-dressed, poorly-nourished, runny-nosed children!

"What utter madness," she sighed in English, smiling at them all the while.

Gladys was now in mountains she had never traveled before. Being off the main trail was very hazardous too.

173

Often the trail was so steep the older children would have to form a chain by which the smaller ones could cling as they clambered up or down. After seven days on the trek the band of children was losing heart. Their feet were sore. They were underfed. They were very tired and cranky. Their clothes and bedding were torn and filthy. Their shoes were nearly worthless rags.

"Soldiers ahead!" yelled one of the older boys who Gladys had sent ahead to scout.

"Don't panic, children," urged Gladys, waving the children flat. "They are probably our Nationalist soldiers."

But she was terrified. The Japanese would show no mercy. They detested the Shansi mountain people more than anyone else. The mountain people resisted them relentlessly. Could she keep the children quiet until she could see who the soldiers were? Perhaps. It was near the end of the day. The children were very tired, more than happy to flop and just gaze at the sky a while. Their little bellies were heaving. They were not frightened. Most had been on the run their entire lives. Gladys crept forward. She peered down at a line of soldiers.

"Nationalists!" she cried.

One moment of supreme dread quickly passed into a moment of great joy. Soon the children were frolicking among fifty soldiers, who treated them with food. The men were well supplied. They even had candy. Candy was almost unknown to these orphans. The children were not resentful or petulant when the soldiers departed the next morning. These orphans had learned how to make small pleasures last. For a long time the memories would be fresh. Why, thinking of candy was almost as sweet as actually eating the candy.

But the pleasurable thoughts finally wore away and soon they were miserable again. Many children had lost their bowls and chopsticks. Many were now barefoot. Their clothing and bedding reeked of human waste. They had been on the trek twelve days.

"The Yellow River!" screamed a scout.

There it was below them, vast and silvery from these heights. The eyes of the children flashed excitement. The journey was virtually over. All they had left to do was cross the Yellow River and catch a train. They had heard Gladys say so. Oh what fun to ride a train!

Gladys thanked the Mandarin's men before they began to walk back to Yangcheng. Then the troop of urchins headed down to the Yellow River. There was no trail but no one minded now. A few hours later they trudged into a village called Yuan Ku.

Only an old man was there. He told Gladys the Japanese now controlled this north side of the Yellow River. He stayed only because fleeing was too arduous for him. If his last act was to spit in the face of a Japanese soldier he was too tired to care.

"But where have the other villagers gone?" she asked.

"To the other side of the Yellow River, of course," he replied.

"Yes, of course. That makes sense. Where can we find a ferry?"

"There are none."

Her heart grew cold.

fourteen

"No way to get across the river?" she mumbled numbly.

Never had she expected this. The river was vast—an impenetrable barrier without a boat. Now it seemed like a trap. Would they wait there until a Japanese patrol found them? Why hadn't she asked the Nationalist soldiers more questions?

She had the orphans camp by the river. The older boys foraged for food in the abandoned village. Gladys prayed. And she tried to reassure herself with human logic. Surely the fifty Nationalist soldiers had come from the south side of the river. So every few days a patrol probably landed somewhere along the bank and every few days the patrol was picked up at some pre-arranged spot. She mustn't lose heart.

"God, protect us," she prayed.

But the days dragged by. The children were not complaining. After all they no longer had to trek through mountains. The more resilient ones were enjoying themselves. As

176

long as they didn't think about how hungry they were they were even happy. But on the fourth day hunger had conquered optimism. Even Gladys was depressed.

Suddenly children began screaming, "Soldiers!"

Once again Gladys had a moment of agony until the soldiers came into focus. Nationalists. Eight of them. They had been observing Gladys and the children for some time. They were almost as young as her oldest boys, so she knew they too probably made good scouts.

The soldier in command of the patrol grumped to Gladys a while about how dangerous it was for her to try to take one hundred children to Sian but as he watched the filthy urchins his complaint died. He shrugged. He probably would have tried the same thing. He signaled someone on the other side with a mirror. A brilliant flash answered him.

"It will take three trips to get all of you across," he said, his eyes scouring the sky. "The enemy planes are usually very bad along this river. They love to strafe harmless innocents. But for the last few days they have been absent. Maybe they think everyone who is going to cross the river has already crossed."

The crossing was successful. Two days later Gladys and the children were in Mien Chih, well south of the river. Friendly villagers fed them, bathed them, and escorted them to the train station the next morning. Trains carried only refugees now.

Of all the trekkers, Gladys was the sickest of all. She felt faint very often but had to ignore it. Did she have another choice?

The children were buzzing with excitement. Not one had

ever seen a train before. When it actually arrived they were aghast. What a smoke-pluming, steam-spewing dragon it was! Everything about a train was loud. Clanging. Wrenching. Hissing. Screeching. Weren't things being devoured by this monster? The smallest children had to be coaxed aboard.

"The train is much smaller than a mountain," reasoned Gladys. "Come aboard. And watch out for splinters!"

The cars were barren wooden boxcars. But the children didn't care. They sprawled everywhere. After the train began click-click-clicking along the track they were enchanted. Soon they were chittering excitedly. The train wasn't so bad. And how their feet hurt from walking. They wiggled their toes and laughed. But the first tunnel threw them into hysteria again. Gladys could only pray one of the little ones wouldn't panic and go running off blindly. But when they came out of the tunnel they were appeased. Then they began to anticipate tunnels and relish them, screaming in delight.

"Oh, Jonah into the whale's belly!" the smallest would scream every time they were plunged into darkness.

Occasionally the train would stop and its passengers could get off and be fed at a refugee camp. But at a small village called Tiensan, Gladys was told the train would go no further. A bridge had been destroyed by the Japanese. She resolved they would simply walk the track as she had done so many years ago in Russia. But no, that was not possible, she was told. The track was squeezed between two mountain ranges, the Zhongtiao on the north and the Xiao on the south. The Yellow River was a torrent there but very narrow and the Japanese could easily shoot them

178

down from the other side.

"But we must get to Sian," she told her informant.

He gazed at the Xiao range looming to the west. "Your only hope is to cross those mountains."

"What is the trail like?"

"I don't know. We never use the trail," he said weakly.

Gladys groaned inside. Those mountains looked more rugged than the ones in Shansi. She didn't know them either. Many of the children were walking on rags now. *Oh God, give me wisdom,* she prayed. *What are we to do?* As if her feet had a mind of their own, they trudged toward the mountains.

Several hours they climbed up a slope. Did the bones of her children ache like her own? Did their muscles scream in pain too? Finally the trail leveled off and they reached a village by nightfall. The villagers welcomed them. Who could resist these brave urchins?

Gladys was apprehensive as the villagers described the trail to her and the other villages she would encounter. It sounded very difficult. But what could she do but trust God? Surely God would protect them. She had not lost one child on the trek so far. But could such tiny bodies keep going with no food?

Their bodies did seem to rebel in the following days. Their heads lolled weakly as they trudged along. Gladys's body was no exception. How tired she was. She was nauseated too. Her head ached. How she wanted to just lie down. At one point on the trail Gladys did flop beside the trail. She broke down and cried. Soon the entire caravan seemed to be weeping uncontrollably.

She forced herself to stand up. "It's good to have a big

cry once in a while," she announced, trying to ignore the hysteria in her voice.

Gladys began to doubt herself. She seemed feverish and confused. What if she had taken a wrong turn? One day they had been descending for a long while. Were they descending into just another intermontane valley? If so, they had another heartbreaking climb ahead of them. Gladys wasn't sure she had the strength to make it. At nightfall they entered a village.

"Are we leaving the mountains?" she cried, not bothering to be polite.

"This is Tong Kwan," answered a villager. "Of course you're out of the mountains!"

Praise God, sighed Gladys. The detour through the mountains was over. But how many more setbacks could Gladys and her orphans handle? What she heard from the first railway official she talked to was like a slap across the face.

"There are no passenger trains to Sian from here," he said. "Even for refugees. Don't you know there is a war on?"

Gladys couldn't bring herself to answer such an idiotic question. The man spoke the tiny thoughts of a bureaucrat. He walked away. She was ready to fall over when another man approached. He too worked for the railway.

"There are coal trains going west," he said.

"Yes?" she acknowledged cautiously.

"They leave after nightfall, so the Japanese have a harder time spotting them. The coal is loaded in an open-topped car called a gondola. If you are willing to take the chance, I will help you and your children climb into the cars. You can ride on top of the coal."

And so they did. God must have had His hands on the children because no urchin toppled out of a gondola during the journey. Gladys wondered how she herself kept from tumbling out of the rough-riding cars.

They left the coal train at a town called Hwa Chow, where the passenger service picked up again. There seemed to be little fear of the Japanese here. The passenger train skimmed along the south bank of the Wei River. Pagodas and walls, some standing and some in ruin, began to appear everywhere.

For hundreds of years Sian had been the capital of China, protected from invasion out of the north by the rugged plateau country Gladys knew so well, and protected from invasion out of the east by the narrow pass through the mountains at Tong Kwan. Her brave urchins had made a journey that had repelled invaders!

Sian was very large and very ancient. Soon the train stopped near the city's north wall, which appeared to extend at least two miles. The wall was about forty feet high with watchtowers on the corners. In the center was an enormous gateway complex of three towers.

"If this north gate to Sian is anything like England's ancient gateways its towers contain many forms of death," reflected Gladys.

But she and the children were not to discover anything about the gateway. Sian was a closed city. They would not take more refugees. Then she learned the other hundred orphans from Yangcheng were not in Sian anyway. They had been diverted to Fufeng, eighty miles farther west.

Gladys seemed lost in an endless maze now. Soon she found herself and her orphans on a train chugging toward

Fufeng. The children were an irresistible force. Everyone tried to resist them at first, but the sight of such sturdy, lovable urchins melted their hearts. Time and again it seemed Gladys was stymied, only to have another opportunity pop up right away. God was surely guiding these poor children! Finally they reached the orphanage in Fufeng.

"You look very sick to me," said a woman at the orphanage.

"Many people have told me that lately," said Gladys.

That was the last thing Gladys remembered for a long time. Even when she regained her consciousness later she felt only half there. "Where am I?" she asked a white-clad woman. "Who are you?"

The startled woman answered, "Why, you're making sense for once!"

Immediately the woman vanished.

Soon a man hovered over Gladys. In English he said, "I say, the nurse tells me you've got your senses back. Jolly good."

"Where am I? What happened?"

"Hold on a minute. I'm a senior physician at Baptist Hospital in Sian. I'll explain it all to you if you'll be silent. You were brought to a mission in Hsing Ping, then here. You've babbled on and on for weeks. No apology necessary. You had a severe fever. One hundred and five degrees. Your brain should have baked. You also had typhus. Pneumonia as well. Yes, and malnutrition too. Exhaustion. And a bullet seemed to have branded the back of your shoulder! Oh well, I only tell you these things, good lady, because I'm certain now you're going to live."

"Are the children all right?"

"Children?"

"I have a hundred children. . ."

"Nurse!" called the doctor. "Bring a sedative."

Gladys was finally discharged. By now she knew she was considered a miracle at the hospital. Only the happenstance arrival of a new drug called sulphapyridine saved her from certain death. Apparently she had helped in various ways with refugees for several months before collapsing at Hsing Ping. Gladys had no memory of that. She had lost about one year of her life.

She was discharged from Baptist Hospital in late 1941. By 1942 she was toiling at the Fishers' Mission in Mei Hsien, which was not far from Fufeng. Many of her children were now in Sian too, so she felt compelled to stay in the area around Fufeng and Sian.

Gladys did not eat well. She did not get enough sleep either. It was no wonder she still occasionally blacked out. She was forty years old now.

The Fishers voiced their concern. "Good heavens, Gladys, slow down."

Gladys refused. Other refugee missionaries stayed with the Fishers. Annie Skau was a Norwegian nurse who had worked northwest of where Gladys had worked. Annie was a mountainous presence—six feet-two inches tall and over two hundred pounds in weight.

"I read my Bible this morning," she told Gladys, who had become pessimistic in her poor health. "God spoke to me very clearly about the Japanese in 2 Kings 19:7. 'Behold, I will send a blast upon him, and he shall hear a rumour, and shall return to his own land; and I will cause him to fall by the sword in his own land.' So there, you see the Japanese are doomed!"

In 1943 Colonel Linnan found Gladys in the Sian area. Gladys had not lost her pessimism. "I hear the Japanese have conquered Tong Kwan. They are at last through the great pass. This jolts me. They are now south of the Yellow River and west of the mountain barrier—the very one I scaled with the children."

Colonel Linnan never lost his composure. "The Japanese attacked America in 1941 and gave their naval forces in Hawaii a crippling blow. But Chiang Kai-shek always believed the Americans would come back even stronger. And the Americans have smashed the Japanese navy at the Battle of Midway. The Japanese will soon have to give only a token effort against China because their effort against America will start draining their resources. We Nationalists would also like to make a token effort against the Japanese." He noted the surprise in Gladys's face. "Yes, this surprises the Americans too. In fact it makes them very angry. But it is because we must save our strength to fight the Communists. They have now raised an army of one million. And the Communists in Russia will supply them modern arms in any way they can."

"Oh no," groaned Gladys.

This coming tragedy she should have foreseen. How many of her trusted friends had predicted such an event? But to think that after Japan withdrew, China would still have war on all fronts—this time a vicious civil war—was heartbreaking. Would the bloodshed never end?

Her feeling for Colonel Linnan seemed no longer the desire of a woman in love but the warmth of a friend. What was it she wanted from Colonel Linnan? Marriage? Or only friendship? It troubled her so much she consulted a cleric. "Either get married or trust that the Lord will satisfy your desires in His own way," he advised.

She thought very hard on it. Colonel Linnan had an ambitious career. He admitted it. A wife who had her own mission among the dispossessed would only tear him apart. And if she gave up her mission she would be torn apart.

"But what does the Bible tell me?" she wondered. "It has all the answers."

Suddenly she remembered Nehemiah's terrible anger against any Israelite marrying other than another Israelite. How could she have hid his righteous rage from her consciousness for such a long time? *Ye shall not give your daughters unto their sons, nor take their daughters unto your sons, or for yourselves. Did not Solomon king of Israel sin by these things?* But did this advice apply to Gladys marrying a Chinese? No. Nehemiah condemned marrying outside one's faith, not marrying outside one's race. So it was not wrong for her to marry Colonel Linnan because he was Chinese—it was wrong for her to marry him because he was not Christian.

Yes, her course of action was clear to her now. "So it's over," she admitted numbly.

fifteen

G ladys spent four years in the Sian area. By the middle of 1944, the Japanese were being pummeled in the Pacific islands by the Americans. Their presence in China was disintegrating. They had never penetrated west of Tong Kwan. Now they were being pushed out of China by the Nationalists, especially in south China. In the north, the Communists were doing little but stockpiling supplies they would need to fight their own countrymen!

Gladys could not sit and reflect on such evil. "I must continue working for Christ. But I am no longer compelled to stay around Sian because of the children. They are all married or working or in schools or in the army."

First she went west to Lanchow, then south to the province of Szechuan. Chengdu was another very large city. The climate was milder than any Gladys had experienced in China. Its bounty from agriculture was much greater. They not only raised wheat and corn but rice, cotton, tea, and much fruit. Chengdu itself was ancient. Like Sian, remnants of older dynasties were everywhere. To their credit the Chinese tried to preserve their temples and pagodas. Often though they were reproductions because the original wooden structures had burned. Gladys heard the surrounding hills and mountains were full of old monasteries.

In 1945 she heard how the Japanese had returned to their own land and "fell on their sword," just as Annie Skau had predicted from her Bible. Although war with Japan was over, war in China continued. Chiang Kai-shek's Nationalists were now fighting the Communists.

Could Gladys survive another national tragedy? For five years now she had lived in tiny rooms, often with refugees. She had no private facilities. Like the poorest Chinese, she used outside latrines and washed up when she could. Her one luxury was a thermos bottle. In the morning she heated water to boiling and poured the steaming liquid into the thermos bottle. All day long she refreshed herself with weak tea. But it hardly sustained her. Pushing herself beyond her strength she still had blackouts.

She worked with lepers now. She was far more than a nurse or a comforter. She brought the hopeless the hope of Christ. Once the most miserable of human beings, her lepers now glowed with their love in Christ. Gladys persuaded a pastor to regularly give them the Sacrament of the Lord's Supper.

"Their bodies are so contorted with disease they cannot kneel," observed the American doctor Olin Stockwell. "Their hands are so crippled they can barely receive the elements. Yet their eyes flame with joy and hope. All because Gladys Aylward brought them Christ."

Once Gladys trekked the heights ramping up into Minya Konka, a peak of Himalayan size only a hundred miles from Chengdu. There she had a mystical experience. She found a monastery hidden on the far side of a mountain, much as her old Bei Chai Chung had been isolated. The monks expected her! Here at long last was the messenger they had waited for, they said. They eagerly accepted her message of salvation through Christ. The whole episode seemed a dream after she returned to Chengdu to work with the lepers and refugees again.

She taught English to eager young students. One pastor gave her a room in back of the church and a regular salary to be his "Biblewoman." For this she did every chore he asked, including cleaning the church building. Always she was busy. Everywhere she was a force.

She was also exasperating to less committed people. Only God and the Bible guided her. She could never account for any money given her. As likely as not she had given it away within minutes of having received it. Always her fellow missionaries tried to slow her down.

"It's not the work that is crushing me," she told cohorts. "It's the fate of my children. I heard my son Less was yanked out of school by the Communists and shot. He's not the only one of my boys who has died for Christ. And my daughter Ninepence is married but I don't know where she is. I don't know if she is alive or not."

The Communists were ruthlessly successful in those years. Russian Communists had leaped into the war against Japan in the final few days to capture large depots of weapons. These they turned over to the Chinese Communists. Well-armed and ever ready to promise peasant recruits the moon, the Communists grew in strength.

The Nationalists under Chiang Kai-shek had a long history of broken promises, thanks to the warlords who would not cooperate with Chiang's reforms. By 1947, except for a few Nationalist strongholds, the Communists controlled all of north China. Nationalist China was about to collapse. Gladys too appeared about to collapse.

"Gladys, you've been here in China for seventeen years without a furlough," scolded Dr. Olin Stockwell.

"But I am a Chinese citizen."

"Still, you must go visit your parents in England at least. And rest."

She was penniless, so Stockwell raised the funds. Some money was his own and some money came from a missionary fund for abandoned missionaries. "Who deserves it more than Gladys?" he argued.

But more than funds was required. Gladys was officially Chinese. So she whiled away months at the China Inland Mission in Shanghai waiting for a visa. Thousands were fleeing China. But God gave her a great surprise in Shanghai. She found Ninepence!

"And I am a grandmother—because I am certainly grandmother to Ninepence's toddling son!"

It was spring of 1949 before Gladys found herself back in England. Her parents, her sister Violet, and her brother Lawrence were all alive. Yet she had problems adjusting to life again on 67 Cheddington Road. As often as not she chattered Chinese at astonished English faces. Sometimes she was uncontrollably morose, as if overcome once again by the torment she had suffered for nearly twenty years. The deaths of so many of her beloved children and China's impending collapse to Godless Communism tore at her heart.

"Poor, poor China," she lamented.

The news from China was all bad. The Communists, who would stoop to anything to win, prevailed. Chiang Kai-shek and his remaining army were exiled to the large island of Formosa. Gladys realized with a start that if she ever went back to China it was only the China on that island of Formosa that was open to her! She also realized that all the missionaries were gone from China. Or if not, they were in prison—like her dear benefactor Olin Stockwell! And what of the Mandarin? She would probably never know. And what was the fate of Colonel Linnan? Was it any wonder she became morose?

But Mum never relented trying to get her active again. "Gladys, won't you speak to our ladies' group in Hoxton? And don't you worry about your English!"

Suddenly Gladys recalled noting in the margin of her Bible: "promise of March 1949." It referred to Luke 21:15. She read the passage again: *For I will give you a mouth and wisdom, which all of your adversaries shall not be able to gainsay nor resist.* God would help her, as He always had. She just needed faith.

Strange and wonderful things began to happen. Her command of English returned. Her love of the stage, lost since childhood, returned. Her compulsion to preach returned. She began giving talks.

How she enjoyed surveying her audience with her mousiest look, while announcing in her most quaint voice, "Now the Lord said to Abram. . . ," then rattling the windows with,

" 'Get thee out of thy country, and from thy kindred, and from thy father's house, unto a land that I will show thee.' " Few were not stunned by her force. And it did no good to tell her to hold her talk to fifteen minutes or to half an hour. When Gladys spoke it was for at least one hour and usually longer. She was called by the Lord to speak this way. She had her strength back.

She loved to speak in metaphors. "God had a man, well-educated, strong, handsome, as talented as one of the Cambridge Seven, all lined up to go to China in 1930. But one of those great mysteries in God's plan happened. The man was not available. So God looked around and saw a simple London parlor maid, homely, poor, and ignorant— *but willing!*" And she liked nothing better than to startle her audience. Finger jabbing at them she would shout, "Look inside your own hearts and see if you are *willing* to obey God!"

A newspaper journalist Hugh Redwood began writing about her service in China. One day another journalist, Alan Burgess, came to visit her on Cheddington Road after reading one of Redwood's newspaper articles. Burgess was writing and producing a series for BBC radio on war heroes called "The Undefeated." War heroes? *How nice,* thought Gladys. But how could she help him? She didn't really know any war heroes herself. General Ley, maybe. Well, they didn't have to be war heroes in the strictest military sense, suggested Burgess. Heroes of great courage.

"Perhaps David Davis. . ."

"What about yourself?" he asked. "Surely you must have had an adventure or two over there." But his face was shrouded in doubt.

Gladys felt mousier than ever. "Me? I've done nothing the people who listen to BBC radio would think interesting."

"Did you come into contact with Japanese?"

"Well, yes." She hid a smile. She knew Alan Burgess would have been impressed if she told him she had been shot down in a field outside Tsechow. Bombed too. In Yangcheng. Strafed too. Smashed in the head once with a rifle butt too. "Some of the Japanese are very nice, you know," she said.

"I see you led a rather sheltered life in China." Still he pressed her. "Surely you must have experienced some adventure there?"

She shrugged. "My fondest memory is taking some children to an orphanage in the area around Sian."

"Really?" he said, not bothering to hide his disappointment. "Children? To an orphanage?"

"Yes, it was across some mountains."

"*Across* the mountains?" He perked up. "Real mountains?"

"Yes, I think you would call them real mountains. The trip was made more difficult because we couldn't use any main trails. Oh, and we had to cross the Yellow River too."

"Isn't that the terribly dangerous river that floods so often it's called 'China's Sorrow'?" Alan Burgess grew more and more animated as Gladys recalled her adventure. Finally he looked numb. He mumbled, "No food. No money. Just you and one hundred children for one month of travel across mountains, across rivers, through Japanese patrols. Under Japanese dive bombers. And you were sick with fever and typhus and pneumonia and malnutrition? Yes, Miss Aylward, I think BBC might be able to use your story."

Gladys was invited to a rehearsal at a studio in the Picadilly area of London. There she met the very distinguished cast of actors. Playing her was Celia Johnson, a noted actress of the time. And yet the cast seemed more in awe of her than she was of them. Gladys was amazed at such a reaction.

Her father had come with her, and now he said nervously, "I came with my little Gladys because of the frightfully heavy traffic around here. I don't like to think of my little Gladys crossing the street alone."

Gladys enjoyed the BBC production, even though it made her part too heroic. Then a small booklet about her by R. O. Latham publicized her exploits. She resolved never again to encourage such self-praise. She continued to speak, but privately, she lamented the fact that her Chinese was getting rusty.

Her knowledge of Mandarin was much too valuable to waste. Soon she was helping at a hostel in Liverpool for Chinese seaman and refugees. She campaigned for cast-off clothing to be sent to refugees in China.

Alan Burgess returned to Cheddington Road to tell Gladys that the publisher Evan Brothers had offered him a contract for a book about her. Was she willing? Gladys could tell he expected her to refuse. She had soured on all the praise earlier. She herself expected to refuse. But suddenly she accepted. It was another way to keep interest in China going among the British. So Burgess interviewed her for four months. She was never more aware of her blackouts from 1940 to 1949 than when she tried to recall what she was doing and when and where. And she was not good with dates anyway.

"Oh yes, I was born for certain on February 24, 1902," she volunteered perkily, "but after that. . ."

"Dates are not critical," he reassured her. "It's your wonderful story that counts. I'll do the best I can to confirm dates for what you've told me and sort it all out."

He told her he would need months to write the book and then it would go through editing with the publisher. She forgot about the book. She had far too much to do. Then precious Mum died. How it jolted Gladys. Mum dead and Gladys herself now fifty! Gladys must get on with her work. She had been in England too long! By the time the book came out in 1957 Gladys had already reserved passage on a ship to Hong Kong. She had little interest in the book. When some company called Twentieth-Century-Fox wanted to buy the movie rights she signed them over to them with scarcely a thought.

"Well, if you're so foolish as to pay good money for the story of a little parlor maid. . ."

sixteen

Hong Kong confirmed to Gladys that China was like all Communist countries. People were trying desperately to get out. No one tried to get in—except for Gladys. And yet her beloved country was barred to her. For a while she watched in bewilderment as refugees flooded into Hong Kong from China.

But then Gladys found "Michael," one of her children who had crossed the mountains with her. He was now a minister. With Michael and his wife Maureen, Gladys quickly hatched a plan to begin a mission in Hong Kong for refugees.

"We will call it the Hope Mission."

But Gladys was denied a resident visa. She was a citizen of China. There was only one place she could go: the island of Formosa, Chiang Kai-shek's Nationalist stronghold.

Although Formosa was but a tiny microcosm of mainland China it did not seem insignificant to Gladys. The mountainous island was twice the size of Wales, half as large as Scotland. By 1957 Formosa was already a show-case of what all of China could have accomplished under Chiang Kai-shek's Nationalist rule. It was popular to call Chiang the "man who lost China," but Gladys knew in her heart China was the loser.

Formosa was separated from mainland China by a hundred miles of rough sea and one century of modernization. Mainland China—or "Red China"—was lost in totalitarian madness. The Formosans of "Free China" were building roads and industry. All citizens were being taught to read and write.

"Chiang Kai-shek has declared that all Formosans must become fluent in one language: Mandarin," mused Gladys.

So Gladys immediately became a teacher of Mandarin. Formosa welcomed her with open arms. She met Madam Chiang Kai-shek and thanked her for the orphanages she had set up during the war. Gladys found several of her children: Jarvis, Francis, and Pauline.

She finally settled in Tapei, living in her frugal way. Then orphans started coming to Gladys. She attracted orphans like a magnet. She was startled. She was now well past fifty. Would she have the energy? She had her doubts, but God had no doubts.

"Surely He is the one gravitating these orphans toward me," reasoned Gladys.

People began talking about the book called *The Small Woman,* written about her by Alan Burgess. The impression given Gladys was very favorable. Then they began talking about the movie that had been made of her great mountain adventure during the war. The movie was called not "The Inn of Eight Happinesses" but "The Inn of the Sixth Happiness."

The decision to change a lovingly-crafted name into one that emoted better was her first inkling that Hollywood had filmed her life they way they wished it had happened. The beautiful Swedish film star Ingrid Bergman portrayed Gladys. German actor Curt Jergens was Colonel Linnan.

"People seem to enjoy the movie very much," a friend reassured Gladys.

But when innocents began asking her questions after seeing the movie, she realized her life story had been mangled almost beyond recognition. Hollywood had her arriving from Liverpool to be rejected out-of-hand not by the China Inland Mission, but by the China Missionary Society. Hollywood had her working not for Sir Francis Younghusband, but for a Sir Francis Jimmerson. Hollywood had Jimmerson condescending to write "his old friend" in China, Jeannie Lawson. Hollywood had entirely removed Gladys's family from the story. In the movie her harrowing train ride across Russia was no worse than a few rude soldiers. Hollywood's train delivered her neatly to Tsientsin!

"Oh, that movie!" she began to sputter if it was mentioned.

Ninepence became Sixpence in the movie, and not her first child but her last. Yang had been made into a comical non-believer in the movie, and then killed off in a touching death scene! The memory of poor Less was besmirched too by calling him "Lin" in the movie. The more she learned of the movie the more distraught she became. Colonel Linnan was portrayed not as a full-blooded Chinese but an exotic mixture of European and Chinese. And very cynical besides.

More and more of the movie was transmitted to her. "There are love scenes!" gasped Gladys.

She was not called Ai-Weh-Deh for no reason. Gladys was the "Virtuous One." She had never kissed a man in her life. To hear that she was shown all over the world in that way mortified her. And the movie ended with her dumping the orphans at Sian so she could rush off to join Colonel Linnan, apparently to "live happily ever after." Oh, what would her friends think? Would they think she had concocted such a silly romance story about herself?

She was inconsolable. She wrote her friends to forget about her. She was disgraced. She just wanted to sink into oblivion. Why had she ever signed a movie contract? She felt like such a simple-minded fool.

"But Gladys," some reasoned. "People don't believe everything in a Hollywood movie. Your friends know you didn't go live with Colonel Linnan after the war."

"The movie is lie upon lie upon lie," she grumbled.

The movie certainly made millions of people all over the world aware of Gladys Aylward. By 1959 she had been invited to America by World Vision to do a speaking tour. She resolved to go in spite of her disgrace. Maybe she could set the record straight. Besides, she couldn't miss a chance to spread the Gospel.

Crowds came to her, expecting to see a tall, gorgeous woman who looked like Ingrid Bergman. What they saw instead was a tiny severe-looking middle-aged woman in a Chinese gown. Their faces soured with disappointment. But God was definitely helping her. When she began talking, their disappointment turned to astonishment. Smashed in the head by a rifle butt? Shot in the back? And what had those in the audience suffered for Christ? Inspired by God she worked them over in her rough way, trying to hammer their blobby faith into something better.

Still, there were hardheads who came up to her afterwards to gush, "Have you ever met Ingrid Bergman?"

Worshipping celebrities—even her unworthy self—was something new to Gladys. It disgusted her. And she didn't hide her anger at such silliness. She snapped rage at such questions. Only Christ should be worshipped!

Still, she persisted. Funds for her work in Formosa were being raised in this way. She even was invited to speak in Australia and New Zealand. In England BBC did a "This Is Your Life" television program on her. Being reunited with Violet and Lawrence was no great surprise to her, but she was stunned to see David Davis again.

This was followed by meeting the Archbishop of Canterbury, then Queen Elizabeth herself. At Buckingham Palace the queen took her into the garden, chatting pleasantly, and pointed out the flamingoes they kept. Gladys, of course, did not miss the opportunity to ask the queen for support.

"The orphans in Formosa desperately need help," she said.

Certainly Gladys had her share of woe. She was vulnerable to any cheat. She had always cared nothing about money for herself and gave money away to the needy as fast as she got it. But her operation in Tapei had grown and Gladys had no talent for bookkeeping. A trusted subordinate at her orphanage embezzled funds. She was as humiliated by that as by the movie. It nearly broke her. What did she possess other than her virtue? Where could she hide from notoriety? It seemed she trusted no one now but God. What human being could she trust? She must not disintegrate into an angry old lady like poor Jeannie Lawson. Then Gladys remembered a large, comforting presence.

"Annie Skau!"

Gladys rushed off to Hong Kong to see her old friend from the war years. Among the charitable enterprises Annie Skau managed was a tuberculosis clinic she called "Haven of Hope." Although Annie focused on medical aid to the poor she had also taken in orphans by the hundreds. She too had endured the war years. She too had suffered under the Communists. She too was a faithful servant of God.

There were few people more in tune with Gladys's own thoughts. Annie Skau insisted Gladys convalesce at her facilities. "Trust God," said Annie when Gladys finally left.

When Gladys returned to Tapei she found waiting for her an English woman named Kathleen Langston-Smith. Kathleen had been a postmistress in Nottingham, England. Watching Gladys on "This Is Your Life" she been overcome by a desire to do what Gladys was doing. She had resigned her job, sold her home, and sailed for Tapei!

"Have you worked with children before?" asked Gladys in her blunt manner.

"No. I've never been married. And I was an only child. But I can do bookkeeping."

"God knows I need help on that front!"

Kathleen Langston-Smith was more than a bookkeeper. She showed great skill in managing the orphanage. Gladys was sure Kathleen was sent by God so that she could retire from working with children. At sixty years of age she did not have the strength. Her body had suffered much from war and from missionary work. Besides that, she was still depressed at times, a dour presence that love-starved orphans didn't need. Nevertheless she cared for a new "son," a mischievous orphan she named Gordon. She had taken Gordon when he was a mere five days old.

She returned to England in 1966 but the attention she received as a celebrity was unnerving. But it did relieve her of one anxiety. "Perhaps I didn't permanently disgrace myself."

In England Gladys was reunited with Alan Burgess. Burgess was pragmatic about how Hollywood had mangled *The Small Woman,* his book about Gladys. He shrugged. The movie was about the best effort Hollywood could make with a missionary's life. Would Gladys allow him to update *The Small Woman* for a new edition? Gladys agreed, and also poured out more details about her early life. Perhaps this revised edition could correct some of the many inaccuracies engendered by the movie, for the memory of the movie still stung her.

Back in Tapei she resumed her work, although it was more curtailed than in the past. Kathleen mothered her into less activity and better health.

"You must take care of yourself," insisted Kathleen.

Sometimes when Gladys reflected on her life—for at long last she had leisure time to indulge in reflection—she could not believe her own experiences. Had that been the parlor maid Gladys tumbling from the second floor of a Chinese inn after a bomb blast? Had that been Gladys dodging soldier's bullets outside Tsechow?

"How God rewarded me with adventure just because I was willing!" she cried.

In the first days of 1970, Gladys awoke with what she thought was a severe cold. In spite of Kathleen's protests, she kept a speaking engagement at a woman's club in Tapei. She returned to the orphanage so exhausted she tumbled into bed. Kathleen called a doctor, who determined Gladys had the flu.

Gladys's mind drifted to Nehemiah. Nehemiah, the servant, had always been her special Bible hero. It seemed that she too had restored a few walls, built a few gates. She too had resisted intimidation. But even Nehemiah's work was finally done.

"Oh God, 'spare me according to the greatness of thy mercy,' " prayed Gladys, quoting Nehemiah, but then she prayed his very last words, " 'Remember me, O my God, for good.' "

Later that evening in January, Gladys Aylward, 67 years old and totally expended, joined the Lord.

Further Reading

I. Two biographies are based on personal interviews with Gladys Aylward:

Burgess, Alan, *The Small Woman.* Leicester, England: F. A. Thorpe (Publishing) Ltd., 1969. Large print revision (with update) of *The Small Woman.* London: Evans Brothers Ltd., 1957.

Thompson, Phyllis, *A Transparent Woman.* Grand Rapids, Michigan: Zondervan, 1972.

II. References on Other Missionaries in China:

Barr, Pat, *To China With Love: The Lives and Times of Protestant Missionaries in China 1860-1900.* Garden City and New York: Doubleday & Company, 1973.

Gleason, Gene, *Joy to My Heart: The True Story of Annie Skau, Medical Missionary to China and Hong Kong.* New York: McGraw-Hill Book Co., 1966.

Steurt, Marjorie Rankin, *Broken Bits of Old China: Glimpses of China 1912-1923.* Nashville: Thomas Nelson Inc, 1973.

Stockwell, F. Olin, *Meditations From A Prison Cell.* Nashville, Tennessee: Upper Room, 1954.

III. Other Helpful References:

Eunson, Roby, *The Soong Sisters*. New York:
   Franklin Watts, Inc., 1975.
Hahn, Emily, *Chiang Kai-shek: An Unauthorized
   Biography.* Garden City/New York:
   Doubleday & Company, 1955.
Hook, Brian, ed., *Cambridge Encyclopedia of
   China,* Second Edition, Cambridge University
   Press, 1991.
Younghusband, Francis, *The Heart of a Continent:
   A Narrative of Travels in Manchuria, Across
   the Gobi, Through the Himalayas, The Pamirs
   and Chitral, 1884-1894.* New York: Charles
   Scribner's Sons, 1896.